The
WISDOM
of
AMERICAN
INDIAN
MYTHOLOGY

by
John J. Ollivier

TOP OF THE MOUNTAIN PUBLISHING
Pinellas Park, Florida 34664-2244 U.S.A.

TOP OF THE MOUNTAIN PUBLISHING
P.O. Box 2244
Pinellas Park, Florida 34664-2244 U.S.A.
Fax (813) 391-4598
Phone (813) 391-3843

Copyright © 1995 by John J. Ollivier

Library of Congress Cataloging-in-Publication Data
The Wisdom of American Indian Mythology by John J. Ollivier.
p. cm.
Includes bibliographical references and index.
ISBN 1-56087-049-4 : $17.95
1. Indians of North America.2. Folklore—North American Indian. 3. Mythology, North American Indian. 4. Proverbs, North American Indian. 5 Legends — North American Indian. I. Title
PS3565.L544W57 1995
811'.54–dc20   95-9359 CIP

Cover and text design by
Powell Productions
Painting *Dakota Mist* by
Frank Howell

Manufactured in the United States of America

TABLE OF CONTENTS

Cover and text design by Dr. Tag Powell
Powell Productions

OTHER WORKS BY AUTHOR JOHN OLLIVIER
Fun With Nursery Rhymes
Fun With Greek Myths
Fun With Irish Myths
The Wisdom of African Mythology
The Wisdom of American Indian Mythology
The Wisdom of Nordic Mythology in 1996

OLLIVIER'S CHILDRENS WORKS INCLUDE:
My Friend the Dentist
What Funny Little Ears Can Do*
Thumbs Are Not Dumb*
Tick Tock Clock*
* illustrated by Mark D. Smith

The Wisdom of American Indian Mythology

PROLOGUE

The Indians we've come to know
    Are myths of western fiction,
Who speak their thoughts in grunts and groans
    And "ughs" of Tonto diction.

We've pictured them as savages
    That white men tried to tame.
We thought we had to steal their land
    To fill this noble aim.

We stole their land and sent them off
    To arid reservations.
And somehow history justified
    Our moral aberrations.

We whites have been the savages,
    Though this we won't admit.
There were no crimes nor cruelties
    That we did not commit.

The Spanish soldiers stole their gold;
    The English stole their land.
The Frenchmen stole their pelts and skins
    For beads of glass and sand.

Whites have rewritten history
  To justify their deed,
A form of self-deception
  To vindicate their greed.

It's only in their ancient myths
  That red men can be known,
Where values and their family life
  Became life's cornerstone.

And so we'll search these ancient myths
  To grasp the red man's mind.
And I am sure that as we do,
  We'll see that we've been blind.

We'll see their sense of sacredness
  And love of natural beauty.
We'll see a sense of honor that
  So venerated duty.

We'll learn of Indians suffering,
  But faithful to their word,
In spite of broken treaties
  And fork-tongued things they heard.

We'll see the white men confiscate
    The lands and woods they loved,
And hunt and kill their buffalo,
    A gift from God above.

In spite of these adversities,
    They never lost their pride.
They fought for what was rightly theirs,
    And fighting, many died.

But white men still don't understand
    How wrong past deeds have been.
They somehow look upon those deeds
    As if there were no sin.

It is our hope that in this book
    Such views will be recast,
And whites will come to disapprove
    Their plunder of the past.

The Wisdom of American Indian Mythology

FOREWORD

This scholarly work on *The Wisdom of American Indian Mythology* is directed as much to the White Man's attention as it is to the Indian's pride. Many whites know Indians only from unhistorical movies of the Wild West which depicted Indians as ruthless savages on constant warpaths, and whites as the innocent victims of the Red Man's savagery. Much of this antiquated prejudice was handed down by fur traders, pioneers, and cavalrymen. Seldom did white men hear the voice of the Indian himself, and even on those rare occasions when the Indian's voice was heard, his words were twisted and their meaning distorted by the lips of white men who served as interpreters.

We must know what the American Indian WAS to know what the American Indian IS. We must know the Indian of the past to know the Indian of the present. He was not the Hollywood stereotype. He was not the ruthless savage of American myth. He was rather the gentle and farsighted spiritual person of Indian mythology. He was the person who loved and valued nature as a gift God entrusted to us and for man's wise and proper use.

Indians were not the wild and ruthless savages depicted by an arrogant Andrew Jackson or by an egotistical maniac like George Armstrong Custer. Indians were rather the "tractable and peaceful people" Columbus proclaimed us to be.

Not only are white men often times ignorant of Indian history, but the Indians themselves are frequently unfamiliar with their own heritage and culture. As children they were often placed in Indian schools, not to learn of past glories and ancestral ways of Native Americans, but to learn the glories and ways of the white man. As the Sioux Medicine Man, Leonard Crow Dog, so wisely pointed out, Indians were "Whitemanized." This created the dangerous situation in which their marvelous native culture was all but forgotten.

Today there is a steadfast reaction to this whitemanization of Indians of every tribe, fostering a growing interest and pride in their history and culture. This is especially true among younger American Indians. The young are determined to resist any further encroachment upon their past heritage and they are resolute to right past wrongs. Unfortunately, however, this determination is often based upon an enthusiasm and emotion rather than upon a knowledge and understanding of past glory.

A study of the ancient mythology of American Indians will give Indians of every age that needed knowledge and understanding. It will acquaint them with the history of their ancestors as they struggled unto death against the forces of nature and against the oppression and greed of the white trespassers. When all Indians, young and old, grow in their knowledge of past glories, then will Native Indian pride grow ever more deeply.

Native American Indian mythology flows from the world of nature. The howling winds, the babbling brooks, the buffalo chase, the plains and the forests, these are the stuff of their legends handed down over the centuries by their ancestors from one generation to the next. A study of that mythology will give both Indians and white men a glimpse of the social order and daily life of a culture too easily forgotten. As in the ancient past, these tales are told not just for the enjoyment and pleasure of the listener. They are told to keep alive Indian treasures and traditions that will link Indians today to past ancestors and cultures... and to foster in Native American Indians a justifiable and much needed pride.

The Wisdom of American Indian Mythology

It is impossible to do justice to the immense richness and variety of Indian mythology in a single book, but the author, John Ollivier, makes a splendid effort to do so. The historical background needed to understand the myth is set forth in prose and then the myth itself its told in a delightful and often times witty limerick. It is my hope that his work will contribute to the growing interest and appreciation of American Indian culture in our world today.

Dr. Tag Powell
Publisher

INTRODUCTION

In any study of Indian culture or Indian religious beliefs it is impossible to speak of Indians in general. Indians in general simply do not exist. The English poet, William Blake, once wisely warned that to generalize is to be an idiot. We must heed his prudent caution and avoid the trap of generalization in any cultural or religious study of native American Indians. All Indians are different. They have different histories, different languages, different cultural values, and different religious beliefs. The uniqueness of the individual tribes must be understood as a given, if we are to understand the richness of American Indians today.

When Columbus landed in the New World there were about a million Indians spread throughout what is now known as the United States and Canada. In that space there were six hundred distinct Indian nations, each complete, self-reliant and self-governing. There were twenty-nine million Indians living in South America. South American Indians gave way to slavery, North American Indians would not. They chose war. They yielded only to the sheer fact of being physically overwhelmed by mechanical forces and numbers.

All Indians were divided into tribes. Few tribes numbered more than a thousand members. They were kept small for purposes of hunting game which was often scarce in given locations. Because tribes were small, religious ceremonies were designed for small groups. Today tribal membership is determined by federal law which lists tribal membership numbering in the thousands. This fiction of the federal government has done much to wipe out the Indians' ancient beliefs and past tribal practices.

The tragedy of this federal interference is not that beliefs have been discarded and practices abandoned; the true tragedy is that they have been forgotten. Some current Indian activists insist that Indians today cannot be fully Indian unless they actually relive their past beliefs and follow past customs. They deny that it is sufficient to know and respect past glories. This is like saying that an Irishman cannot be fully Irish unless he believes in Druids and banshees, or that a Dane cannot be fully Danish unless he worships Thor. Every race must respect its past glory and still recognize that progress can be made in any given culture. No race nor culture must be enslaved by what happened hundreds of years ago.

Just as Indians of the past readily adopted the horse, when it was introduced by Spaniards, without losing their identity, so, too, Indians of today can adopt the automobile or the pickup truck without selling out their cultural heritage. They can accept the God of the Christians without condemning or debasing the beliefs of their ancestors. The reason for any change or refusal to change is far more important than the change or the refusal itself.

Long hair symbolized the Indian's identity, his independence, his sense of superiority, and his sense of pride. To the Puritans, wearing long hair was a symbol of pride. The Indian's long hair was an affront to Anglo-Protestant Christianity that figured the Indian was civilized only if he suppressed his independence, his native habits and instincts, and dressed and acted like Europeans. But to the Indian, a willingness to cut his hair signaled his desire to kill the Indian in himself and assume a new person modelled after the white man.

To the English, Indians stood against all that the English stood for, all that was good, Christian, and civilized. To the English the Indian was immoral, pagan, and barbarous, and so they tried to remake the Indian through education in school and in church. For instance, if an Indian child in the white man's school spoke his native language or sang Indian songs, he was actually flogged. They were forced into an existence which was confusing. Frequently, the Indian child did not know who he was or where he belonged. White schools made Indian children ashamed to be Indian. This was tragic as well as cruel.

White Europeans came here looking for freedom of speech and freedom of worship. No sooner did they find it in this land than they themselves denied it to the natives who had dwelled here for centuries.

It still seems strange that white men are so intent upon saving whooping cranes and the spotted owls, but have little interest in saving Indians. The American policy toward Indians has always been assimilation or extinction. Indian children should be proud of their heritage. They are Indians. An understanding of their past is vital to a sense of pride in the present. Yet there has been a concerted effort carried out over many years by soldiers, teachers, missionaries and bureaucrats to obliterate Indian history. "The victors write his stories; the vanquished are rendered historyless."

The Indians' history was oral. Indians had no written language. But in the foolishness of the white man, oral history was non-history, a bundle of superstitions without value which stood in the way of Europeanizing native Indians. Histories written by white men were unjust to Indians. White victories were called battles; Indian victories were called massacres. Those histories never mentioned that Indians fought in defense of their lands, their hunting grounds, their forests, their buffaloes, and their sacred burial grounds. White men who rise to protect their property are called patriots; Indians who do the same are called savages and murderers.

White men called Indians treacherous, but no mention is made of the hundreds of broken treaties on the part of white men. White men called Indians thieves, yet it was the white men who stole the Indians' land. White men called Indians savages, yet their religion was noble, their art original, their music stirring, their legends rich. William Penn wrote of Indians in 1683: "They do speak but little, but fervently and with elegance. I have never seen more natural sagacity." These so-called savages taught their children to love nature, not abuse it. They killed game only for food, never for fun.

Indians were friendly to white settlers and taught them how to survive in a hostile environment. In turn, whites treated Indians shamefully.

Indians are a proud and independent people. Can we condemn them because they did not want to be governed by another race. Before the white man came Indians were happy. There were many buffaloes to eat. Indians could come and go like the wind. When it grew cold they could journey to the warmth of southern valleys, and when it grew warm they could travel to the mountains of the north. Then white men came and killed their buffaloes and deprived them of their tribal customs and ancient freedoms.

Yes, white men stole the physical things that Indians held dear, their lands and forests and food. The most devastating and lasting plunder inflicted by the white man was the privation of their Indian heritage and culture through a deliberate and calculated process. As a consequence, many modern Indians are unfamiliar with the glories of their past and the myths and legends which formed that past and contributed so much to their ancestors' pride.

It is the intent of this work to study those ancient myths and present them to Indians so that they can retell them to their children in a way that children can understand. In so doing it is further hoped that the roots of past glories may contribute to the splendor of the present and the grandeur of the future. In his fine work, *The Indians of the Americas*, John Collier writes:

> "To know the spirit of the Indians of the United States is to know another world. It is to pass beyond the Cartesian age, beyond the Christian age, beyond the Aristotelian age, beyond all the dichotomies we know, and into the age of wonder, the age of dawnman. There all the dichotomies are melted away: joy requires sorrow, and sorrow, joy; man and society and the world are one: fantasy and the old, hard wisdom of experience join in the rituals, the moralizing tales and songs, the myths. Idealism and ideality are joined with searching and undeviating practicality. And the child is joined with the man."

THE INDIAN CONCEPT
OF THE LAND

The red man with his straight black hair
   And features broad and strong,
And copper-toned complexion
   Was happy, not headstrong.

Then white men like voracious fiends
   Came crying out with greed.
"We want your lands, your homes, your game,
   And care not if you bleed."

"We even want your sacred grounds
   Where ancestors are buried.
What you won't give We'll take by force,
   Then send a missionary."

The Indian can't understand
   The white men or his creed,
For land's not owned by any man.
   Great Spirit holds its deed.

He made the stars and universe,
   The grasses of the field.
All things on earth belong to Him
   And everything they yield.

Their God is older than their needs
    And older than their prayers.
And in His generosity
    The earth with them He shares.

The Indian could never sell
    That which no man can own.
If he would try such foolishness,
    His God he would dethrone.

The Black man said he had a dream
    Of freedom in this land.
The red man had no need of dreams,
    For this land bore his brand.

And yet the red man still had dreams,
    Of things that brought him joy.
Great fields of maize and streams of fish
    And hunting with his boy.

His dreams soon turned to nightmares, though,
    And joys turned into sorrows.
And hopes gave way to deep despair
    And "Wounded Knee" tomorrows.

The white man who was civilized,
    Then brutalized the savage.
He changed his name and dress and cult,
    All signs of white man's ravage.

Whites made him farm instead of hunt,
    And from his past depart.
The red man might have scalped the head;
    But white man scalped the heart.

And this continues to our day,
    As white men never learn.
Whites think they know the red man's thoughts
    Whose culture they still spurn.

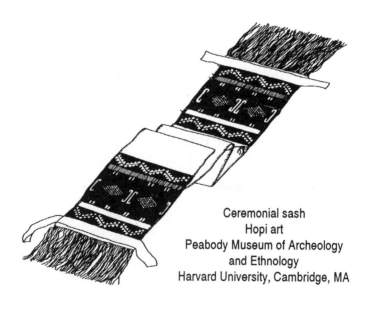

Ceremonial sash
Hopi art
Peabody Museum of Archeology
and Ethnology
Harvard University, Cambridge, MA

THE VALUE OF MYTH

The ancient myths of the Native Americans have been told and retold for thousands of years. Tribal myths embody the collective experiences of an entire people, their successes and failures, their movements and migrations. By transforming past happenings into the sphere of myth or legend a people can celebrate or mourn its past, honor its heroes, and encourage its youth to future glory.

Myths are like special glasses through which we can view the social order and daily lives of a past people. Through the study of a people's myths we can discern how their society was organized and how their government was structured. We can look into their religious ceremonies, their family life, the values that were treasured, how members of society dealt with one another, what they ate, what they fought for, and how they celebrated festive events. Myths are studied not just to entertain, but to instruct. Myths were the beliefs of a past people. They were a living religion. As Bunislaw Malinowski so rightly said: "Myth in its living, primitive form is not merely a story told, but a reality lived."

The world of myth is a world of powers and forces. What white men called inanimate objects, the Indians found pulsating with life, like rocks and mountains, and rivers. Nature is but a collision of those powers which compose it. Indians developed a religion to help them cope with these powers, to deal with the unknown, to face the mysterious, to seek protection from the supernatural universe whose powers everywhere surrounded and threatened them.

It can be said that myths migrate as easily as people for they accompany them wherever they go. And so although their cultures were diverse, Indians developed an interrelated and complex religious structure and an elaborate system of ritual and ceremonialism that rested on such elements as Mana, taboos, animism, visions and superstition. Mana was the name of the forces pervading the universe with power to influence places, things, and human beings.

The religion of the Indian was not essentially monotheistic. Indians believed in a supreme being who was good and an opposing spirit that was evil. In his spiritual vision the Indian saw himself not as the highest creature and lord and master of all others. He rather considered himself the brother of life. Through the practice of religion man sought not so much to control himself, but the world about him.

The religion of the Indian was a private affair. Indians did not proselytize. They vested others with the duties and works of religion. These were known as shamans, priests, and prophets. They dealt with the spirit world and were considered conjurers, wizards, medicine men, healers, and workers of magic. They were thought to possess special powers over men, animals, and the forces of nature. The unseen spirit world of gods and demons was responsive to their power. They could subdue all things by incantations and ritual. Their influence was sought to bring victory in war, to bring rain upon crops, to drive out evil spirits, and to control the unpredictable forces of nature.

The shaman acted for the entire group. He used magic drums to arouse violent emotions in warriors. Many religious rites, music, and dancing in colorful regalia were devoted to appeasing or petitioning the gods who controlled the forces of nature.

Different tribes held various beliefs concerning the next world. Some referred to future life as a "Happy Hunting Ground." Some saw heaven as the home of the Great Spirit. Others saw it as an escape from the miseries and wretchedness of this life. Some believed in several heavens, one for warriors, one for women, one for the aged.

All tribes had creation myths to explain the origin of things: how the physical world came to be; what was the origin of corn, of salt, of the buffalo; why men and women differ; what was the source of evil. Indian myths, like all myths, were the result of primitive, but reasoning minds seeking to know the causes of things. No mind can close itself to the question of causality. Indians were no exception.

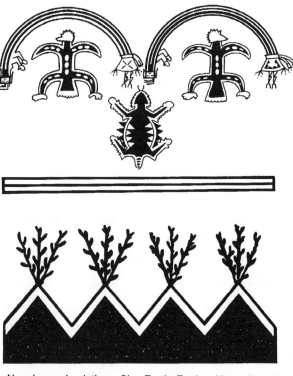

Navajo sand painting—Sky, Earth, Eagles, Horned toad
Wheelwright Museum of the American Indian, Santa Fe

GLUSKAP AND MALSUM

According to Algonquin tribes,
    Two brothers made all things.
From Gluskap comes whatever's good,
    From Malsum evil springs.

Kind Gluskap made the fertile plains,
    Plants, animals, and man.
While Malsum made all snakes and bugs
    To fit his evil plan.

Since Malsum hated every good,
    He sought his brother's death.
He planned a means whereby he could
    Deprive him of his breath.

He told Gluskap in confidence
    Fern roots would make him die,
And wondered if this same strange fate
    To Gluskap did apply.

Gluskap said "no" and Malsum asked,
    What possibly could slay him.
The unsuspecting Gluskap said:
    Owl feathers could waylay him.

It wasn't long till he was hit
By feathers from a bow,
Shot by his brother Malsum,
Who caused the fatal blow.

So Gluskap died and fell to earth,
But by his magic rose,
And realized to only one
Death's secret he'd disclose.

Then Gluskap mentioned to a stream
How luck avoided doom,
For lasting death could only come
From reeds that were in bloom.

A toad then overheard him speak,
And sped off as a spy
To tell this news to Malsum
And asked for wings to fly.

But evil Malsum would not give
The toad the power of flight.
He said a toad with wings would be
A rather silly sight.

The toad in anger then sped off
    To Gluskap telling all,
Who sought a fern with deep large roots
    To heed toad's warning call.

In anger Gluskap hurled the root
    Which stuck in Malsum's head.
His magic powers were driven out
    And Malsum now lay dead.

He could not rise as Gluskap had
    Revivifying life.
So he became a cruel wolf,
    And since has caused man strife.

Then Gluskap finished all his work,
    Creating all creation.
The beauty of the universe
    Which won man's admiration.

With work now done he climbed into
    A birch-bark small canoe.
He travelled to the sunrise then
    And bid the world, "adieu."

Now as we greet the rising sun,
  It's Gluskap that is greeted.
They say one day he will be back,
  When he again is needed.

We all must face the rising sun
  And get on with our lives,
We must achieve our destinies,
  Before our time arrives.

One day we must board our canoe
  And paddle to the sun.
And as we leave our lives on earth,
  May nothing be undone.

We must complete our present tasks
  And serve this world's Great God.
Our moccasins must walk those paths
  Where our forefathers trod.

Hohokam art
Arizona State Museum
University of Arizona, Tuscon

IN THE BEGINNING

Indians had a very deep appreciation of the natural world. There was an old Sioux saying that: "All things are tied together with a common navel cord." To Indians all things were somehow one. They viewed themselves as brothers and sisters to streams and mountains and corn. They were one with the bear and buffalo and even with the deceitful coyote. The birds were cousins and the smallest insect was looked upon as a relative. All things were somehow one.

White men see man as the master and conqueror of nature. Indians, who are much closer to nature, know better than to make such a claim. They recognize the debt they owe to the world around them. They see themselves not as masters of nature but sharers in a noble partnership with it and with the animals of the earth. In olden days, before the white man invaded their land, Indians were even closer to the animals. Many felt they understood the language of animals and could talk to birds or gossip with butterflies. They had the ability to change themselves into animals and animals could change themselves into people. There was a oneness in all life.

Indians believed in TAKUSKANSKAN. Takuskanskan was the power of motion. It animated things and made them live. Indians believed the earth was once human. The Great Spirit made her to be the mother of all people. She was endowed with Takuskanskan. The earth, they believed, was still alive, but changed. The soil was her flesh; rocks were her bones, the wind was her breath, trees and grass were her hair, and when she moved about, Indians witnessed an earthquake.

When the Great Spirit changed the mother of all into the earth, he gathered some of her flesh and rolled it into balls. Those balls became the ancients of the early world. Some were people. Some were animals which walked like people; some walked on all fours. Some flew like birds; some swam like fish. All had the gift of speech. After that the Great Spirit made balls of soil like Indians, blew on them and made them live. They were ignorant and helpless in the beginning. They were made male and female so they could breed. Thus all things came from the earth. Earth is our mother. She is everywhere.

These first people were very ignorant. They knew they had to hunt and kill in order to eat, but they didn't know which creatures were animals and which creatures were human. Sometimes they ate people by mistake. So the Great Spirit sent the coyote to teach Indians how to live. He travelled the earth teaching the Indians of different tribes how to do wonderful things. In coping with the difficult environment in which he lived and facing the threat of constant warfare from enemy tribes, the Indian gradually developed a virile, structured, brave, and noble personality. The external insecurity which constantly confronted him led to an inward security, a will to live dangerously while living in an impassioned tranquility. One's own fate and life were of no great importance to the Indian. This would be demonstrated in a thousand ways once the greed of the white man challenged the Indian and stole his land. Indians would learn through suffering that human peace and happiness is always at the mercy of fools.

Many today cannot understand the attitude of the Indian. The Indian wants freedom from the white man rather than to be integrated with him. Indians are rugged individualists. Societies were organized only to keep order in camp or on hunts. Indians want to be free to raise their children in their own way, to be able to hunt and fish and live in peace. They want to live off the land, to live with nature as they have done for centuries. They don't want to be barbers or salesmen or congressmen. They want to be themselves.

In the Indian's view of things, time was and is and always will be. It flows like a river. It does not stand still like a lake. In this world view of things, children learn what grandparents know and a culture is handed down from one generation to the next. Religious truths are learned from listening, and ceremonies are learned from watching. Dancing and music are part of religious pageants which act out the spirit of seasons and celebrate the good things of life. Death is but an integral part of that life and in some ways should be used to improve it. This insight is brought out in the following myth.

Sikyatki pottery design
Southwest Museum, Los Angeles

CORN AND A MOTHER'S LOVE

When god, All-Maker, lived on earth
    There were no people there.
Then suddenly a boy appeared,
    Born from the sun's warm glare.

This boy was motion of the winds,
    The moisture of the wave,
And as the sun's warmth fell on him,
    Life's energy it gave.

Then one day soon a girl appeared
    From dew warmed by the sun.
She said: "I am the nourisher,
    Who'll care for everyone."

The boy and girl were married then,
    And she became First Mother.
She brought her children into life,
    First one and then the other.

As population's numbers grew,
    The hunting game decreased.
And as that game grew scarcer,
    Starvation soon increased.

First Mother grew disconsolate,
    As children to her crept.
"We're hungry, Mother, feed us, please!"
    But lacking food, she wept.

"Be patient, I will make some food."
    She sadly said through tears,
Then called her husband to her side,
    And whispered in his ears.

"I have a favor I must ask:
    Dear husband, take my life."
Her husband said: "Impossible!
    I cannot kill my wife."

"You must," she said, "And God agrees.
    Tomorrow at high noon!
And let me now assure you,
    That will not be too soon."

"When I am dead have our two sons
    Take hold of my dark hair,
And drag my body 'cross the land
    Until my bones are bare."

"Then take my bones and bury them
Amid some lovely field.
And after seven moons come back
And see what I shall yield."

And as was asked, the deed was done.
First Mother had been killed,
Her body dragged till bones were bare,
Just as First Mother willed.

Her husband wept as did the sons,
But still her wish did grant.
Then after seven moons came back
To find a noble plant.

It was a tall and tasseled plant.
The Mother's flesh was maize,
Which she had given in her love,
To feed men all their days.

They tasted it and found it sweet,
And nourishing to life.
It fed her hungry children then
And wiped out future strife.

First Mother had instructed sons
  To set aside some corn.
And put its kernels in the earth
  For races yet unborn.

Then where they buried Mother's bones
  Another plant soon grew.
This was the first tobacco plant
  That anybody knew.

Tobacco was her breath of love
  As sweet corn was her flesh,
Fine gifts she gave us in her love,
  That daily would refresh.

So as we smoke her sacred plant
  And feast upon her grain,
Let each of us recall her life
  That for us has been slain.

First Mother was the font and source
  Of every mother's love.
A love as noble and as good
  Must come from up above.

So treasure what this universe
    Has given us in love.
The world and all its blessings are
    A gift from God above.

We must avoid all wastefulness
    Of gifts that nature gave.
How tragic to destroy those things
    That future men will crave.

I think we all must somehow learn
    Before those gifts are gone
To love the blessings nature gave
    And red men have passed on.

The future will look back to us
    And judge us by our deeds.
Did we pass on earth's flowers
    Or just confer its weeds?

Pueblo pottery design
Private collection

INDIAN WOMEN

An old Sioux proverb says: "Women shall not walk before men." In many ways the Indian woman was subservient to man, but in many ways her role was as important as the brave's. Indians believed that it was the work of a woman's hands and the fruit of a woman's body that kept the world alive.

Lakota Indians were considered to be the purest tribe among the Sioux and so the White Buffalo Woman, the most dominant figure in Sioux legends, gave them the sacred pipe which holds all things together. It was this pipe that bound men and women together in a circle of love. It was used as a symbol of marriage binding men and women together for life.

Although the White Buffalo Woman first appeared to the Sioux in human form, she was also a buffalo, the Indians' friend that gave its flesh so Indians could live. The White Buffalo woman was the Spirit that took the form of a maiden buffalo dressed in buckskin to help Indians. She gave the tribes great herds of buffalo, taught them how to worship and cook and marry. When she finished teaching them she walked away, rolled over and became a black buffalo, then a brown one, then a red one, and finally the sacred white buffalo calf. The albino buffalo was especially sacred to the Plains Indians. It was the Buffalo Woman that taught women to fire the hearth and cook corn and meat, and to weave baskets.

Women do all the cooking in an Indian village. Indian males left most of the work to women. Indian men were chauvinists, by modern standards. Any work that seemed womanish, like cleaning fish, they refused to do. They lived by what pleased them, like hunting and fishing. Farming, although done to some measure, especially by women, was never very important or stable. Stable farming threatened their independence. If done, they could not pull up stakes and move.

The Indian woman's labor, however, was not more severe than the labors of a white woman and her cares were not half as numerous. The spinning and weaving and sewing that colonial women did was unknown to Indian women. Harvesting corn was the work of the women. Planting corn was the duty of men, while shawl-shrouded women chanted songs to encourage men to work and seeds to grow. It was felt that without the woman's chant seeds would not bear fruit.

Iroquois accorded a position of considerable importance to women. Women did not speak or vote in council, but they had the power of veto. The consent of all women who bore children was needed before important measures could be taken. Candidates for chieftain were nominated by the vote of mothers. The clans of the Iroquois were matriarchal. They reckoned descent from the mother, not from the father. An Iroquois woman had as much right to divorce her husband as he had to divorce her. The house and all possessions, other than tools and weapons and clothing, belonged to the woman.

The Algonquins were also matriarchal. Among Pueblos the dominant figure was the mother's oldest brother. It was he who was responsible for the lives and training of his sister's children. It was to him that children went for counsel and correction. The father could correct but he could not punish. His authority was over his sister's children. A husband lived in his wife's house from which he could be ejected. In that case he returned to his mother's house.

Indians have many myths about men and women, how they came to be and how they first came to dwell with each other. The Navajo tribes believed the gods wanted to make people more like the gods. They had bodies like gods but teeth and feet and claws like beasts and insects. Also the men had very bad body odor. They were told to be clean when the gods would come in twelve days. On the twelfth day the gods appeared carrying two ears of corn. The white corn became man; the yellow corn became woman.

The following myth describes how men and women first came to enjoy each other's company after their creator had made a mistake and placed them in the universe at such a great distance that they never knew each other existed.

Anasazi art
Peabody Museum of Archeology and Ethnology
Harvard University, Cambridge, MA

MEETING AND MATING

The Old Man made the universe
　　And everything within,
But he had made a great mistake
　　That caused him much chagrin.

He had placed women far apart
　　From where he had placed men.
And so these two had not yet met,
　　Not since the world began.

The men had learned to make the bow,
　　While women learned to tan.
The women dressed in buckskin clothes,
　　But never met a man.

One day Old Man said to himself,
　　I've made a grave mistake.
For men and women do not know
　　The joys they could partake.

So Old Man went to visit them
　　And saw fine tents and clothes.
Then women went to spy on men
　　And problems soon arose.

The women saw men poorly dressed,
    Unwashed and dirty skinned.
And so they warned the kind Old Man
    Man's presence would offend.

And when the men repaid their call,
    The women had been tanning.
They smelled of blood and carcasses
    For meals they had been planning.

Men saw the women standing there,
    With knives in bloody hands,
The men then thanked their lucky stars,
    They lived in other lands.

The Old Man knew he had been wise
    To place them far apart,
For ugly, smelly lady friends
    Could never win man's heart.

The women had been victimized,
    The timing was not right.
They knew that women tanning skins
    Were not a pretty sight.

And so they thought they'd try once more.
They bathed and braided hair.
They dressed in dazzling doe skin clothes,
Which caused the braves to stare.

The men went to the river's edge
And bathed and rubbed on fat.
They put bright feathers in their hair
To play aristocrat.

The women came all singing songs,
Quite pleasing to man's ear.
The men now saw their loveliness,
Rejoicing they were near.

The women too then realized,
These men were not uncouth.
To say they found men pleasing,
I think would be the truth.

It wasn't long till they paired off,
Each woman and each man.
And marriage then soon followed,
According to love's plan.

These men and women joined in love
    And happiness they found.
And as they shared in sacrifice,
    Their love grew more profound.

The women cooked and tanned for men.
    The men all hunted game.
They shared their life and shared their love,
    And we should do the same.

In this way families came to be,
    The first the world had known.
And children soon were born to them,
    The future's cornerstone.

There are some things that each of us
    Could gather from this tale.
Impressions that are first observed,
    So seldom will prevail.

Sometimes we may not look our best,
    Like when we tan a hide.
But that which really matters most
    Is that which is inside.

When things are viewed from distances,
    We miss the things that count.
The things we think most useless
    Are often paramount.

So take another look at things
    That you have set aside.
And you will find their usefulness,
    If eyes are opened wide.

The Indian learned from these myths
    Great truths to guide his life.
They served him as a helping hand,
    Like hatchet or his knife.

And each of us can learn the same,
    If we'll just look around.
These myths will lead us to a fount
    Where wisdom can be found.

Pueblo pottery design
Private collection

THE BUFFALO

The Indian lived in the wilderness. They never built towns. They were a mobile society in constant search for food of game and berries. Indians depended totally on their physical environment. They moved in the winter for warmth and in the summer for mountain breezes. A village of a hundred wigwams could move overnight to parts unknown. It was for this reason that Europeans could not control them or predict their behavior.

The Great Plains, which stretched from Texas to the glacier fields of Montana and from the Mississippi River to the Rocky Mountains, were inhabited by a variety of Indians. To the south there were the Commanches, Kiowas, Cheyennes, and Arapahos. To the north there were the Sioux, Crow, Northern Cheyennes, Assiniboines, Gros Ventres, and Blackfeet. These nations were divided into tribes. In the early 19th century the Plains Indians numbered 250,000. They all hunted in the boundless spaces following great herds of buffalo that at one time numbered twenty million.

When there were conflicts over hunting grounds one nation fought another. The Pawnee killed the Navajo, the Comanche killed the Apache, the Arapaho killed the Utes, and the Sioux battled the

Crow. Fighting served to unify a tribe. It also served as a means for young braves to demonstrate valor.

The life of the Plains Indians was centered around the buffalo, and they used every part of it. Its meat was used as food; its brains were used to soften skin; its horns were fashioned into spoons and cups; its shoulder blade was used as a tool to dig and clear the ground; its tendons served as thread and bow string; its hooves were made into glue for arrow feathers; its tail and hair were used as rope; its wool was made into belts and ornaments; and its hide was used for tents, shirts, blankets, and footwear.

Because buffalo were too independent to domesticate, Indians had to be nomadic to follow their wanderings. In pursuing buffalo they often met other tribes that spoke an unfamiliar language. Although in many ways Indians were the same everywhere—they mostly had the same color skin, the same shape of body, the same dark straight hair and the same black eyes—they spoke a variety of languages. In the United States alone there were over fifty-five families of Indian languages. To overcome the language difficulty Indians developed a sign language to communicate with other tribes.

Buffalo hunting was totally different before the introduction of the horse by the Spanish in the later part of the 17th century and before Indians possessed guns. Prior to the horse and gun, buffalo were often driven over a cliff or a precipice to kill them. They were skinned and cut up at the foot of the cliff and the useful parts taken back to camp. (Before the horse, Indians used the dog as the beast of burden.)

In 1871, a tanning process was developed to turn hides into leather. Hides became so valuable that buffalo were killed by the hundreds of thousands by professional hunters. They were skinned on the spot and left to rot. In 1873, there were still a million buffalo. By 1883, they were gone.

Railroads ultimately sealed the fate of the Indian and the buffalo forever. Professional buffalo hunters were hired to kill buffalo to feed the railroad workers and the soldiers who protected them. Killing buffalo for their hides became very profitable. A skilled hunter could kill a hundred buffalo a day and do it for several months. The Kansas Pacific Railroad even sold tickets for hunting excursions. In 1871, hides brought a bounty of $3.50. A few years later the slaughter had been so extensive that hides brought in only $1.00. In that time four million buffalo had been slaughtered. The Indians' way of life was ended. They were reduced to poverty.

The rights of Indians were ignored through all this. White men invaded their territory and buffalo trails. When white men shot the buffalo, red men attacked their wagon trains. As pioneers moved west, forts were erected to protect them. Things grew confrontational. It was freedom of movement that gave Indian life dignity and meaning. White men threatened that movement and thereby threatened the manner in which Indians provided for their family. To be restricted in movement would be to lose everything that made an Indian's spirit proud. That is why the concept of reservations is so totally in opposition to Indian ways and Indian dignity.

Zuni shield
Museum of the
American Indian
Heye Foundation
NY

SOME CHARACTERISTICS
OF THE RED MAN

All Indians loved freedom's path,
    Which drew them to some mountain,
Or led them through the woods and plains,
    Then to some lonely fountain.

There they adored the sun and moon,
    While some adored the earth.
They reverenced all created things,
    For red men knew their worth.

Some men called them uncivilized,
    Because they loved to roam
And they hated wigwams white men built,
    Since nature was man's home.

They walked this earth for many moons,
    Advancing toward the sun,
Until life's moccasins wore out,
    And trials of earth were done.

An honest people with no laws,
    Whose village had no jail,
They spoke no lies nor with forked-tongue.
    Uprightness must prevail!

Their weapons were quite simple things,
    Like clubs and tomahawks,
And bows and arrows that would kill
    The animals they stalked.

They travelled in canoes of bark,
    As silently they paddled.
And when the Spanish brought the horse,
    They rode that beast unsaddled.

They lived on maize and kidney beans,
    And fish and flesh of beasts,
And squash and nuts and artichokes,
    Then finish off their feast.

They hunted deer and antelope,
    And buffalo they chased.
They walked this land for centuries,
    Before they were displaced.

Opposing cultures sometimes meet,
    And conflicts often follow.
Conversion was the white man's aim,
    Which red men wouldn't swallow.

The weapons that the white men used,
    The red men thought bizarre.
Who else but timid cowards,
    Would kill men from afar.

The red men would not tremble, though,
    Like trees whose roots are bare.
They fought the men who stole their land,
    For stealing's never fair.

There seemed no end to numbers that
    The white men sent to battle.
They came from far across the sea
    To make the red men chattel.

I'm sure all red men realize
    This continent's been lost.
All treaties have been broken,
    The red men double-crossed.

Though they have lost this land's control,
    They will forever haunt it.
It's consecrated by their blood,
    And Indians should flaunt it.

And when the white men won the West,
    The West they then destroyed.
They slaughtered all the buffalo
    And forests they made void.

The red men then must flee from whites,
    As mist must flee the sun.
No people has been so abused,
    Nor lives been more undone.

Dishonor for a century,
    Was how the West was lost.
Betrayal of the Indian!
    White dignity the cost!

But whites have lied to justify
    The evils they've committed.
And until compensation's made
    Those whites can't be acquitted.

Hopi design for women's shawls
Private collection

THE WORLD OF SPIRITS

Indian mythology was based on the world of nature which was the abode of the world of spirits. The concept of a single god was foreign to primitive Indian cultures. Powers of nature were personified and took revenge when nature was abused. Individual spirits were sometimes seen in visions by shamans, but they were never formally worshipped. These spiritual beings, which the Hopi called Kachinas, were intermediaries between people and the Great Spirit called the Manitou. But early Indian mythology was not well organized into a religious tradition.

All Indians had a special reverence for their forefathers. The roots of their religious beliefs lay in their close relationship with their ancestors, who were always near to help them in some way. Although the religious beliefs of various tribes had many things in common, it would be a mistake to think they were all more or less alike. Because we see in them a common reference to medicine men and peace pipes, peyote and visions, mythological characters and stories, some might lump them all together in some vague animistic belief system. This would be a grave mistake and would ignore the differences among the hundreds of distinct Indian cultures native to this land.

Navajo elders taught that First Man and Woman created the Navajos and gave them a religion. The mythology of the Cree people was based on spirits of the hunt, for the Cree's home was the forest in which both the hunter and hunted lived. As usual, in such a mythology, animals could speak and converse with man. The development of agriculture by Algonquin tribes is accompanied by a more complex mythology in which the sun and planets assisted man with heat and rain in his agrarian efforts to grow things.

The beliefs of Iroquois were more organized than other tribes. Their practices focused on dance and song like other Indians, but their theology was highly complex. The universe was believed to be directed by spiritual powers of a mysterious nature to whom men must constantly pray for assistance and guidance. Offerings must be made to them. Sometimes the victims offered were prisoners of war, but most often they were animals or the first fruits of the harvest.

Indians of the great forests postulated a supreme spirit, all-embracing, but without form and having little contact with man. This was the Great Manitou.

Religion was a living faith to Indian people. It touched every aspect of their lives, from the spiritual to the mundane. Every Indian's life was a religious journey, from birth rite to puberty rite, from marriage rite to death rite. Each tribe had its own beliefs and practices, its own history, language, and animal fables, its own richness and complexity. Indians saw themselves as stewards of Mother Earth who must achieve a balanced and peaceful relationship between the spirit world and the world of nature. We see this achievement in the following myths.

Kachina dolls
American Museum of
Natural History, NY

THE MAKING OF THE EARTH

Deep water covered all the earth,
    Way back in the beginning.
The animals that now exist
    Were in the heavens spinning.

Their home was high above the sky,
    Above the rainbow's ray.
But things got rather crowded there,
    With hardly room to play.

The moose and buffalo and elk,
    All somehow crowded in.
There simply wasn't room enough
    For bears to make a den.

They looked down on the earth below,
    With water everywhere,
And wondered what was underneath,
    The water that was there.

They sent a beetle down to look,
    Who dove beneath the sea.
He surfaced with a dab of mud,
    And earth it soon would be.

Soon magically this mud spread out
    And went in each direction.
The Spirit tied it to the sky
    With cords that made connection.

The mud was wet and very soft
    And couldn't hold much weight.
So birds were asked to fly to earth,
    And mud investigate.

The birds reported back again,
    That mud was still too soft.
A buzzard later flew to earth,
    When it was set aloft.

When gliding low, its wings touched earth,
    And mountains came to be,
And there within deep valleys,
    There'd settle Cherokee.

Then when the earth seemed hard enough,
    The animals descended.
But since there was no sun nor moon,
    Their world of sight had ended.

And so they went back to the sun,
    And dragged the sun to earth,
They said it would die in the west,
    But east would cause its birth.

They now could see, but it was hot.
    The sun was now too near.
The crawfish had its back burned red,
    And all things lived in fear.

And so they pushed the sun away,
    Until it seemed just right,
Where animals could stand its heat
    And still could use its light.

Things now seemed right in every way
    So God could fashion man.
And thus it was that He began
    To carry out His plan.

Then He who was All-Powerful
    Asked every plant and beast.
To stay awake and watch for man,
    For seven days at least.

But only owls and mountain lions,
  Could God's will realize.
And so the gift of sight at night
  Was given them as prize.

It's only they who hunt at night,
  For only they can see.
The prey they seek is sleeping then,
  So planned by God's decree.

The cedar, pine, and holly trees,
  Alone of plants were found
To keep the watch God sought from them,
  So keep their leaves year round.

The Someone Powerful then said:
  "Now let us create man."
He then made man and woman,
  And that's how they began.

The man poked woman with a fish
  And told her to give birth.
Then after seven days had passed,
  A baby cried on earth.

So every seventh day there came
    Another Cherokee.
If things continued in this way,
    Too crowded earth would be.

So the All-Powerful then said:
    "A child but once a year."
That was the law that God set forth,
    To which men still adhere.

And that's the way that Indians
    Thought all things came to be
The earth and sky and animals,
    And even Cherokee.

They knew things had to have a cause.
    Chance couldn't be the tool.
For chance had meaning only as
    Exception to a rule.

So red men knew there had to be
    A cause for everything.
There's nothing that can make itself
    Or be its own lifespring.

That One who was All-Powerful,
     The Manitou or Spirit,
Was simply thought to be that cause,
     So why should red men fear it?

Their brightly colored totem poles,
     Carved from a sturdy tree,
Served as a kind of Pantheon
     That everyone could see.

So on these poles they carved their gods,
     Supreme God placed on top.
These poles served as their coat of arms,
     A kind of family prop.

They reached these gods by tribal rites,
     By songs and drums and dances.
The genius of their shaman's skills
     Sometimes put them into trances.

Sometimes the dancers wore a mask,
     Sometimes they painted faces,
Identifying with each force
     The spirit world embraces.

The Wisdom of American Indian Mythology

The white man often ridicules
　　The customs red men had.
But when white customs are reviewed,
　　The red men's aren't so bad.

To mock the red man's painted face,
　　And still praise modern fashion,
Is simply to ignore the facts,
　　Replacing thought with passion.

A woman standing at a mirror,
　　Is doing just the same,
With lipstick and eye-shadowing,
　　But with a different aim.

It's not done to fight enemies,
　　Or frighten off a foe.
She thinks it will enhance her looks,
　　But little does she know.

And when you see the white men dance,
　　You see the strangest motion.
You'd swear they had been hypnotized.
　　Why else all this commotion?

The Iroquois' dance seems sedate,
    Compared to jitterbugging.
His treatment of his captives mild,
    Compared to modern mugging.

The beating of the tribal drums,
    Were almost unobtrusive,
Compared to our cacophony
    And music that's abusive.

And red men were not savages.
    They killed their game to eat.
The modern hunter shoots that game
    To pamper his conceit.

So take a look at white man's ways,
    Before reproving others.
And you must sadly face the fact,
    That white men hate their brothers.

How else explain their treatment of
    The men of other races,
The black man held in slavery,
    Or jailed in hidden places?

Or how explain the theft of lands
That Indians have lost,
The treaties that were broken,
For land at any cost?

Or how explain our treatment of
The land which we now claim.
Polluting our environment,
But somehow without shame.

Yes, we could learn from Indians
That we must keep our word,
That what we say is what we mean,
If not, our word's absurd.

Zuni mask
Private collection

WHEN ANIMALS WERE THE BOSS

There was a time when animals
  Were rulers over men,
It wasn't men who hunted beasts,
  But beasts who hunted them.

Men lived on greens and berries.
  That's why they were so thin.
And since the beasts ate human flesh,
  That's where we should begin.

There were but two folks left on earth,
  A girl and her brother.
They lived in constant hiding from
  The brutes that ate their mother.

The boy was dwarfed, but not the girl,
  So she did all the work.
She gathered food and cared for him
  Which he thought quite a perk.

She skinned and stretched the hides of birds,
  And made the boy a robe.
The question why they lived alone
  He thought that he should probe.

Consumed with curiosity,
    He set out to explore,
To look for other boys and girls,
    And hoped there would be more.

He walked a long time in this search,
    So he was very tired.
He lay down on the soft, warm grass
    In robe he so admired.

But as he slept the sun grew hot.
    His robe was burned and scorched.
When he awoke, he cursed the sun,
    By which it had been torched.

He swore some day he'd get revenge.
    He swore this would be done.
He asked his sister for a snare,
    So he could trap the sun.

She made a little string from hair,
    But it was far too short.
She then sought out some secret things,
    Odd things of every sort.

He took this homemade magic snare
    And placed it in the sky,
Across the hole where sun would rise
    His wrong to rectify.

And so there was no day that day.
    The night continued on.
There was no light nor heat nor warmth.
    There wasn't even dawn.

The animals who'd eaten man,
    Themselves were now afraid.
The sun's warmth was bound in a snare,
    As debt to man was paid.

They called a meeting to discuss
    What animals could do.
They stated that the largest beast
    Should gnaw the cord in two.

The Dormouse was the chosen one,
    The largest of all beasts.
But she was frightened of the sun,
    Now tethered in the east.

The Dormouse then set out in search
    And found sun's awkward spot.
And as the sun fought to be free,
    It even grew more hot.

As she began to gnaw the cord,
    Her hairs began to smoke.
And as she chewed her lungs were singed
    And she began to choke.

Then finally the cord was snapped.
    The sun was free to rise.
Its heat had charred and shriveled mouse
    Unto her present size.

The bright sun rays had blinded her
    As she gnawed through the cord.
The animals now realized,
    It's man who was their lord.

So since that time man bound the sun,
    He's hunter not the hunted.
The animals who were supreme,
    Now found their powers blunted.

Again we see the Indians
 Involved in causal thought.
They knew that all the things God made
 Should act just like they ought.

The sun should shed its light and heat,
 And must for harmony.
Unless there's order in God's world,
 There's just catastrophe.

This tale from Winnebago tribes
 Is wise, to say the least,
It teaches us unless man rules,
 He'll be food for some beast.

And every man should realize
 How all things act for good.
If we appreciate this myth,
 I think we've understood.

San Ildefonso pottery design
Museum of Indian Art and Culture, Santa Fe

A BAG OF TRICKS

Before the red man walked the earth,
  The winters were quite long.
The sky was black, the earth was white,
  And birds sang not their song.

The sun was hidden by the clouds.
  The animals were freezing.
There was no heat in all the world,
  And things were most displeasing.

All animals were called to meet
  To see what they could do.
No bears were in attendance, though,
  Not even one or two.

The animals then figured out
  The fault must be with bears.
Had they somehow usurped earth's heat,
  And hid it in their lairs.

The animals then organized
  To seek where bears had gone.
They found them in the upper world
  To where they had withdrawn.

They found two cubs left in a house.
    While mother was out hunting.
And then they spotted many bags,
    All made of soft brown bunting.

The cubs were asked: "What's in the bag?
    I ask you to explain."
"One bag has wind, another fog."
    "The third bag's filled with rain."

"And what about the fourth?" they asked.
    "A secret we can't tell.
Our mother would be mad at us,
    And cast on us a spell."

"But she won't have to know," they said,
    "We never will repeat."
And so the cubs revealed to them:
    The fourth bag held earth's heat.

The animals then took the bag,
    Now that they knew its worth.
With all the bears in hot pursuit,
    They headed back to earth.

They found the hole in the sky,
  And all slipped safely through.
They brought the heat back to this world
  Which made all things anew.

When snows were melted by the heat
  Great floods were everywhere.
The animals sought higher grounds.
  But water soon was there.

A giant fish then swam about,
  And all the water drank.
In doing so the fish became
  A mountain red men thank.

That mountain now reminds red men
  That life can flow from death.
Sometimes a future victory
  Might cost our present breath.

All nature then is somehow one,
  This we must not forget.
At times a thing must give its life,
  If it is to beget.

The Wisdom of American Indian Mythology

These ancient myths taught many things
  To Indians who knew them.
The truths they taught brought wisdom's wealth,
  To those who did pursue them.

And to this day myths still will give
  An insight that is wise.
And those who know the things they teach
  Are wise men in disguise.

The myths of red men were the guides
  That taught them how to live.
Those myths that told them of their gods
  Were also formative.

As ancient men learned from their myths
  Perhaps, also, can we.
If you acquaint yourselves with them,
  I think you will agree.

Mimbres pottery design
Museum of the American Indian
Heye Foundation, NY

A LESSON IN SELFLESSNESS

The ancient myths that red men told
    Were like a kind of schooling.
Where young men learned how they should live
    To get life's favored ruling.

These tales were told on winter nights,
    Around a burning fire.
They taught Apaches selflessness
    That young braves should acquire.

And when a tale was finished
    Another was begun.
The one that's given here below
    Was told to each man's son.

There was a woman old and poor,
    Who's grandson cared for her.
He was too young to hunt much game,
    But famine could defer.

He had the name of Drip Nose Boy,
    Since his nose always ran.
But in responsibility,
    He acted like a man.

As he grew up he sought to learn
  The art of making bows.
So he could better help at home,
  This boy with runny nose.

He sought the village artisan,
  Who produced the best bows made.
The craftsman asked why such a lad
  Would like to learn this trade.

"Why do you want to learn this art?
  Is it for self-conceit?"
"No, I would like to shoot a deer,
  "So grandmother can eat."

"And what else do you have in mind?"
  The bowsmith asked again.
"If my bows are as good as yours,
  I'll trade with other men."

"And then I can get clothes for her,
  And possibly a horse.
That's if my bows are strong and true,
  And much like yours, of course."

"And what is wanted for yourself?"
  The question then arose.
"I do not want a single thing,"
  Replied young Runny Nose.

The artisan was silent then,
  For he was well aware.
The skills he had were given him
  In answer to a prayer.

When he was young he'd gone in search
  Of skills to form great bows.
With prayers and fasts he sought those skills
  Which cedar tree bestows.

The cedar tree then heard his prayer,
  And artisan empowered
With skills to make bows strong and true
  From cedar trees deflowered.

A further gift the cedar gave,
  In giving of itself.
The artisan could hand skills down
  To others than himself.

But he could only hand them down,
    When sought for selfless cause.
He could not pass his skills to those
    Who sought them for applause.

The young boy was the first to ask
    Those powers for another.
He wanted them not for himself,
    But for his old grandmother.

The boy was sent on vision quest,
    Four days to pray and fast.
And if the cedar heard his prayers,
    He'd get what had been asked.

The tree had pity on the boy
    And granted his request.
So with the skills of making bows
    The young boy soon was blest.

The Drip Nose Boy worked hard to learn
    The skills the old man taught.
He made a strong bow for himself
    And buffalo then sought.

The hunting party was amazed,
    And asked whence came his bow.
He said that he had made the bow
    That killed the buffalo.

Soon other braves asked him to make,
    A bow for each of them.
And in return there came fine gifts
    That braves bestowed on him.

Grandmother had the best of things,
    Fine clothes and things to eat.
No longer is it "Drip Nose Boy,"
    But "Bow Man" people greet.

So everything will come to him
    Who wants not for himself.
If its for others that he seeks,
    He soon will fill his shelf.

Hopi design for women's shawls
Private collection

THE PRICE OF DISRESPECT

Raweno made the animals,
    And each as it desired,
Giraffes with long necks as they wished,
    And bears with strength admired.

"Everything Maker" now worked hard
    To finish off the rabbit.
He asked the rabbit what it wished
    And it was quick to grab it.

Raweno finished off the ears,
    The long ears that it sought.
It wanted panther claws and fangs,
    To help it when it fought.

It wanted long legs like a deer,
    So it could quickly run.
But things got interrupted,
    With only back legs done.

The owl that was not yet formed
    Was sitting in a tree,
Impatient for its turn, it screeched,
    Almost with blasphemy.

"I want a long neck like a swan's,
  I want an egret's beak.
I want to be a gorgeous bird.
  And must have what I seek."

"Please turn around or close your eyes,"
  Raweno quickly said.
"No one's allowed to watch me work,
  No bird nor quadruped."

"No one can tell me what to do,
  Or make me close my eyes,"
The owl screeched in disrespect,
  And jeered insulting cries.

Reweno then in anger pulled
  The owl from the tree.
He shook it till its eyes grew big,
  And ears were standing free.

He shoved its head into its neck
  And rubbed its back with clay.
The bird that wanted comeliness,
  Was now an ugly gray.

And since Raweno works by day,
    By day the owl must sleep.
It's eyes will open just at night,
    And lonely vigils keep.

The rabbit had been terrified,
    When screeching owl was scolded.
And so it ran off long before
    The gifts it sought were molded.

And since back legs alone are long,
    It hops instead of runs.
It never got its fangs or claws,
    So everything it shuns.

It would have been a different beast,
    If it would not have fled.
All rabbits would be brave and fierce,
    But now they're wimps instead.

The owl too has stayed the same,
    With big eyes and short neck,
And ears on both sides of his head,
    Each standing quite erect.

The owl now stays up all night long,
    The sentence for his crime.
He has to stay awake at night,
    For days are his bedtime.

And each of us must always be
    The victims of our past.
We're chained to past conditioning,
    As long as time will last.

So we must learn to be content
    To be just what we are,
Or else like hares and feathered owls,
    Our lives will grow bizarre.

Sikyatki pottery design
Southwest Museum, Los Angeles

THE BEAR PEOPLE

The early Indians all believed
    In some Lord of the Sky.
And minor spirits who served him,
    As folktales verify.

They thought forefathers could be met
    By visiting the dead.
They could go to the underworld,
    But should not eat its bread.

If visitors would taste that food,
    They never could depart.
This belief relived Persephone,
    Their ancient counterpart.

And others held that animals
    And humans sometimes marry.
Since cubs could be of either kind,
    The tales they told are scary.

Rhapisunt, daughter of the chief
    Of Wolf Clan's everywhere,
One day while walking stepped into
    Some dung dropped by a bear.

She called the bear a dirty beast,
  She'd kill at any cost.
And as she wandered, muttering,
  The princess then got lost.

She met two men who said they'd help,
  And both were very handsome.
So chattering, she followed them,
  But soon would pay the ransom.

They led her to the underworld,
  Where bear slaves mulled about.
These bears dressed up in fine bear coats
  Whenever they went out.

But in or out of underworld,
  Bear People still were bears.
Though when at home they shed their coats,
  That they when out would wear.

The youngest took her to his house,
  Where bear coats hung about.
A woman there befriended her,
  And said she'd help her out.

The woman told the frightened girl
    Just what the girl should do,
And told her bears had stolen her,
    For thinking bears taboo.

The Bear Prince soon would marry her.
    The wedding date was set.
His father was the great Bear Chief,
    Whose heirs she would beget.

Soon winter came and Rhapisunt
    Was found to be with child.
The bears then moved their village to
    A climate that was mild.

Her husband found a cave nearby
    The home where she was raised.
Her family long had thought her dead,
    When all facts were appraised.

They'd found a basket which she dropped,
    And then some prints of bear.
Her family thought she had been killed,
    And gave way to despair.

A shaman now informed her kin,
    That daughter wasn't dead.
In fact, she lived in nearby hills,
    Where she now made her bed.

So hunters went into the hills
    And slaughtered many bears.
But found no sign of missing girl,
    Who now had other cares.

She was about to give the life,
    She joyfully conceived.
And when that sacred moment came,
    She would be much relieved.

Her husband bear then led his wife
    Away from hunter's bow,
Where she could have her baby cubs,
    And they could safely grow.

Her brother and his faithful dog,
    Would not give up the hunt.
He journeyed into mountains steep,
    As dog went on in front.

The dog began to howl and bark,
    And brother knew he'd found
His sister living in the cliffs,
    Discovered by his faithful hound.

The Bear Prince watched from cave above,
    And knew he'd soon be killed,
By his wife's younger brother who
    At hunting was so skilled.

"Tell brother when he takes my skin,
    My bones should all be burned.
Our cubs will turn to humans, then,
    But hold to truths they've learned."

The brother did as prophesied,
    And smoked the bear from cave.
Then with his spear he struck the bear,
    And cave became its grave.

The two cubs followed mother home,
    Where they became quite tame.
At home they took off bear skin coats.
    And little boys became.

When they grew up they realized,
    Bear People were their kin.
So when their mother finally died,
    They put on their bear skin.

They travelled to the land of bears,
    And met each relative.
They joined with them in happiness
    Which ends this narrative.

But there's a lesson you must face,
    And always be aware.
As leopards can not change their spots,
    A bear must be a bear.

So you must never try to be
    The things that you are not.
And if you try, you'll tie yourself
    Into a Gordian knot.

Frustrations then will mark your life,
    And fill it full of cares.
Till you return to what you were,
    Like those two little bears.

So be what you were meant to be.
  Don't be what you are not.
You're doomed to failure if you leave
  Your own appointed slot.

Again we see the wisdom of
  The red man's ancient myths,
That guided him throughout his life
  As moral monoliths.

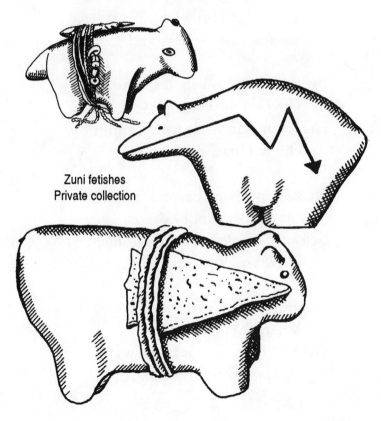

Zuni fetishes
Private collection

TURTLE ISLAND

This land we love and call our home,
 Before Columbus came,
Was known as Turtle Island,
 By Indian acclaim.

It wasn't called America,
 This red man's native land.
They called it Turtle Island,
 A name they understand.

By ancient myth I shall explain
 The part the turtle played.
His loving kindness won for him
 The red man's accolade.

First People lived beyond the sky,
 For earth did not exist.
Below the regions of their home,
 There was just sea and mist.

A gaping hole was in the sky,
 Where they dug up a tree.
The tree fell through as did a girl,
 And landed in the sea.

Two swans swam near to hold her up,
    Or else she would have drowned.
They took her to their Turtle chief,
    Most famous and renowned.

The turtle knew the tree had roots,
    And roots had earth around.
He sent muskrats to find those roots,
    So he could build some ground.

It was a toad that finally got
    A mouthful of that earth.
She spit it on the turtle's back,
    Which soon increased its girth.

It grew and grew till it became
    The island of this world.
It rests upon Great Turtle's back,
    From which it was unfurled.

But it was dark. There was no light.
    And light must be to see.
So Little Turtle volunteered
    To find light's master-key.

She climbed the paths that led above
    The earth into the sky.
She gathered lightning as she went
    And formed the sun on high.

And then she made a smaller ball,
    And it became the moon.
The one would reach its height at night,
    The other at high noon.

The sun and moon were man and wife,
    And sometimes they would fight.
The moon then pined and shrunk in size,
    And gave but little light.

Then after rains when sun would shine,
    The rainbow made a bridge,
The deer was first to climb the sky,
    And walk along its ridge.

Other beasts then followed suit,
    And climbed the rainbow stairs.
They now are constellations like
    The Big and Little Bears.

The woman who fell through to earth
  Was pregnant and had twins.
The first born caused all evil,
  The second, good begins.

Taweskare was the evil one.
  He killed his mom at birth.
He undoes good that Tsentsa does,
  And calls his mischief mirth.

Tsentsa made fine trees and shrubs,
  Taweskare put on thorns.
Tsentsa made a cow's head smooth,
  Taweskare put on horns.

There's good and evil everywhere,
  And red men knew its source.
Tsaweskare made the serpent,
  Tsentsa made the horse.

So some things are considered good,
  While other things are bad.
Sometimes we don't know which is which,
  For nothing's iron clad.

All Indians were pragmatists.
  The good was that which pleased.
The bad was what disturbed or hurt
  Like pain or when diseased.

The modern man still thinks like that.
  He has no absolute.
He only seeks what pleases self,
  Which leaves him destitute.

In some ways he's uncivilized,
  This modern man we know,
No better off than savages,
  Who lived so long ago.

Our hope is that he'll realize
  His life has little meaning,
Until he lives for things worthwhile,
  With values intervening.

Zuni fetishe
Private collection

SCALPING FOR VALOR

There are some today who maintain that scalp-
ing was not of Indian origin. They claim the prac-
tice began in the Massachusetts colony which
offered a bounty of forty pounds for the scalp of male
Indians and of twenty pounds for the scalp of a fe-
male or a male under twelve years old. In 1755, the
Massachusetts's scalp bounty was more valuable
than bounties on beavers and otters. Some main-
tain the Indians adopted scalping in retaliation.
Such a position is simply untenable historically.
There is no word in any Latin or European language
for scalping till 1769. Hangings and disembowel-
ing and beheading were common in European war
cruelties, but never scalping.

In 1535, Jacques Cartier was shown the skins
of five heads of his men stretched on a hoop by
Indians in Quebec. In 1540, two of De Soto's men
were seized by Indians and scalped. In 1549, a cap-
tured missionary was scalped near Tampa Bay. A
companion wrote that he had "seen the scalp of the
crown of the monk." It was the custom of Indians
to flay the head of an enemy and hang it insultingly
on a pole as a trophy. In 1603, Samuel Champlain
was invited to a feast with local Indians who had

just defeated the Iroquois. They danced with the heads of a hundred Iroquois on poles. Champlain records how Indians mutilated their enemies' heads, arms, and legs, and collected the skin of their heads. In 1623, Gabriel Sagurd wrote that the Hurons carried scalps as trophies. Indians had a special word for scalping, to "lift the scalp."

According to Dr. Herman Reas of the Smith Clinic in Marion, Ohio, colonial text books of surgery described the care that should be given those who survived an Indian scalping.

> "After carefully washing the scalped head, superficial burr holes were drilled through the outer table of the skull permitting blood from the diploic space (between the outer and inner tables of the skull bones) to bleed out over the outer table. Since the flow of blood from the diploic space is very slow, the blood would coagulate in the holes long before there was any danger of the patient bleeding to death. This blood would then coagulate and form a scab and protect the underlying bone from infection."

When wars were fought nearby, victors cut off the head, hands and feet of the conquered and brought them back to the village as a prize. The practice of scalping developed as a means of carrying a trophy home from wars that were fought far from one's own village. Scalping was considered a special trophy for it required a definite skill to do and an elaborate preparation of drying and stretching. A fire was lit right after a battle to dry the scalp. Their was a special Indian call or yell when the scalp was taken and another when it was carried home. At home the scalp was placed on a coup pole and Indians danced around it. For each coup a warrior received an eagle feather. The war bonnet, then, was not just a gaudy headdress. It was earned plume by plume.

The bloody possibility of having one's scalp ripped off to a heart-rending cry by a frightfully painted, half-naked warrior was terrifying to the colonists. But to the Indian this was not savagery but the proof of valor. Without the scalp their tales of victory would not be believed. The scalp was the symbol of prowess and bravery in battle. Indians also believed that the soul or living spirit dwelled in the top of the scalp. To scalp the enemy then was to totally degrade him.

THE ORIGIN OF SCALPING

In prehistoric Indian times
    Nesaru governed all.
He was in charge of all those things
    That walk or creep or crawl.

And here is how things came to be,
    So very long ago,
When he was living in the sky
    With only seas below.

Two ducks were swimming in the sea,
    Two men gave this command:
"You ducks dive to the bottom,
    And bring up mud for land."

And this they did, and those two men
    Made earth for God's elite,
Great prairies for the animals,
    Great hills for human feet.

These two then went beneath the earth,
    And there two spiders found.
They taught these bugs to procreate,
    Which they did underground.

The spiders made the animals,
    And then a giant race.
The animals praised Nesaru,
    But giants slapped his face.

Nesaru then created maize,
    And sent its seeds below.
They grew into a smaller race,
    That wouldn't cause him woe.

The giants he destroyed by flood
    Deep underneath the earth.
All others things he brought above,
    And recognized their worth.

He sent Corn Mother down below
    To set his people free.
But in the earth's deep darkness,
    Not one of them could see.

And in this darkness all things groped
    And scrambled on in fright.
The badger tried to dig a hole
    But failed to reach day light.

The Wisdom of American Indian Mythology

The mole who dug to reach that light
    Was blinded by its rays.
It burrowed back into the ground,
    And that's where it still stays.

A long-nosed mouse then cracked earth's crust,
    But broke its large, long snout.
All mice now wear a nose that's short,
    For helping things get out.

They followed trails that led them west,
    Its wonders to partake.
The owls led when night set in,
    And loons led 'cross the lake.

Then Nesaru appeared to them
    To talk a little shop.
He held a staff within his hand,
    With captured scalps on top.

He taught them how to cure disease
    And how to please their god,
And how to sacrifice white dogs,
    Which we might think quite odd.

The Wisdom of American Indian Mythology

He taught them how to offer smoke
    From ripe tobacco plants.
He taught them how to dance and hunt,
    And how to sing war chants.

He taught them how to wage a war,
    Or live in peace instead.
He taught them tribal honor,
    And how to scalp a head.

By scalping heads the braves would show
    The courage red men need.
And this would point to future chiefs,
    Who future tribes would lead.

I'm sure some think this barbarous.
    At least they think it's cruel.
The practice seems so heartless that
    We're quick to ridicule.

But we who think we're civilized,
    Will scalp in other ways.
We grasp at opportunities
    That decency betrays.

We think that we can further selves,
    By running down our neighbor.
As if our idle words could be
    A substitute for labor.

A reputation then is scalped
    Instead of just a head.
And often times we harm man more
    By rumors that we spread.

Most men prefer to lose their life,
    Than live their life in shame.
They'd much prefer a scalping than
    To lose their family name.

Nor can we ever counteract
    The gossip that we spread,
For there are those who'll always believe
    Most anything that's said.

Mimbres pottery art
Maxwell Museum of
Anthropology
University of New Mexico

DESCENDANTS OF THE EAGLE

Of all the tribes upon earth
    The Sioux tribes are most regal.
For only they, of all red men,
    Descended from the eagle.

And this is how it came to be
    So many moons ago.
And then they handed down this myth,
    So future Sioux would know.

When this great world was newly made,
    Unktehi caused a flood.
That monstrous dragon of the sea
    Sought everybody's blood.

Sea waters rose to mountain tops,
    And covered every peak.
Then people climbed up rocky heights,
    That safety they might seek.

But waves crashed them against the rocks.
    Their blood made those rocks red.
And still today red rocks are signs
    Of ancestors long dead.

When quarried now for smoking pipes,
　　Those stones are sacred yet.
The red bowl is ancestral blood,
　　That's now a calumet.

The stem's the backbone of dead kin.
　　The rising smoke's their breath.
When used in ceremonies,
　　The rite recalls their death.

Unktehi, too, was turned to stone,
　　Her bones now form the Badlands.
Her back became the long, high ridge,
　　Which has replaced pine-clad lands.

But when death's call claimed every life,
　　One girl escaped death's jaws.
A giant eagle swooped to earth,
　　And took her in his claws.

He took her to the tallest tree
　　Within his Black Hills home.
It was the only spot on earth,
　　Not covered by sea's foam.

The eagle, Wanblee, loved this girl,
　　And she became his wife.
And when the given time had past,
　　She brought his twins to life.

His tree became a tree of life.
　　As she bore girl and boy.
So people lived on earth again,
　　Which brought their mother joy.

The waters soon receded when
　　The winds began to blow.
So Wanblee placed his family
　　Upon the land below.

He left his children all alone,
　　Now standing on dry land.
"Become a nation that is great,"
　　Was Wanblee's last command.

The eagle's wish was realized,
　　As they begot the Sioux.
And when that noble race was born,
　　The world began anew.

All Sioux can trace their origin
    To this majestic bird,
Which is the source of all their pride,
    At least that's what I've heard.

The eagle is, of all the birds,
    The wisest and most strong.
That's why for Sioux in peace or war,
    Things seldom will go wrong.

And that is why Sioux fighting braves
    Would wear the eagle's plume.
It pointed out past heritage,
    And voided future doom.

Now everyone should wear with pride,
    His heritage and source.
The fool alone regrets his past,
    And views it with remorse.

If one's embarrassed by his birth,
    Though it be high or low,
He's worth much less than even thought,
    So little does he know.

We don't judge men by what they have,
But rather what they are.
For things they have can disappear,
Just like a falling star.

If men have placed their hope in things,
They're doomed to deep despair.
For often when they look for them,
They'll find they've gone elsewhere.

So rearrange your values now,
And be a noble race.
Be ye from eagles or from crows.
Your birth is no disgrace.

Express your thanks to all of those
Who formed your early years.
And as you do, be wise enough
To shed some grateful tears.

Ancient Pueblo
pottery design
Private collection

A BRAVE YOUNG GIRL

Before the white men ever came
    The red men fought each other.
The war of ancient enemies,
    Was brother fighting brother.

The Mingoes were a cruel tribe,
    With numbers like the sand.
There was no way to battle them
    If they attacked full-manned.

One day they charged Oneida tribes,
    And set their homes afire.
Oneidas fled into the hills,
    Till Mingoes would retire.

Oneidas hid among the rocks,
    But soon ran out of food.
They wondered how they could escape
    The Mingoes that pursued.

A young girl then addressed the chiefs.
    She said she'd had a dream.
Her name was Aliquipiso,
    Whose dream revealed this scheme.

"We're hiding here among the rocks,
  With boulders all about.
If we could lure our foe beneath,
  We'd win without a doubt.

"We'd hurl these boulders down on them.
  And crush them where they stand.
We then could go back to our homes,
  And repossess our land."

"But how can we entice our foe,
  To fall into your scheme?"
The chief asked Aliquipiso,
  Who then explained her dream.

"Sir, I, myself, shall go below,
  Pretending I am lost.
And I shall lead them to that spot,
  Where they'll be double-crossed."

Her courage that Great Spirit gave
  Was highly praised by men.
They knew that she would lose her life
  And not be seen again.

So in the darkness of the night,
    The girl walked to and fro.
The Mingoes found her wandering
    In wooded lands below.

They said that they would spare her life,
    If she'd betray her tribe.
Adoption by the Mingoes
    Was added to the bribe.

The girl pretended to disdain
    The bonus they proposed.
But when they tortured her with fire,
    They found her more disposed.

She led them through the silent woods
    And over winding path.
She led them to the towering cliffs
    And to Oneidas' wrath.

She said Oneidas slept above.
    The Mingoes drew nearby.
She then cried out the warning sign,
    And rocks flew through the sky.

So many Mingoes died that night
    They ceased to be a threat.
Oneidas since have lived in peace,
    And in the maiden's debt.

And where big boulders covered her,
    Sweet honeysuckle spread.
And to this day that bush is called
    "The blood brave women shed."

Her courage and her sacrifice
    Are told each year anew,
Where underneath the rocky cliffs
    This maiden won a coup.

I'm sure that some will not agree
    This maiden was heroic.
I'm sure some think her quite a fool,
    And certainly not stoic.

They'd say that men just let her die,
    So each of them could live.
And then they spread her foolishness
    By myth and narrative.

By praising her, men could deceive
   All future generations,
Enticing women to perform
   All kinds of aberrations.

They say that men are chauvinists,
   That's what they have decreed.
All selflessness is weakness!
   And love's not in their creed.

There's no such thing as sacrifice
   Or laying down one's life.
They simply cannot understand
   The love of man and wife.

Because of this, I am convinced
   Some will disdain this story.
They simply do not understand
   Love's power or its glory.

Mimbres pottery design
Museum of the American Indian
Heye Foundation, NY

MEDICINE BUNDLES

Two hundred years ago the Great Plains of North America were covered with huge expanses of grass that stretched out for nearly a thousand miles. That expanse was intersected by rivers and valleys along which Indian families lived and grouped themselves into tribes. Although some of those tribes cultivated maize and beans and squash like the Iroquois in the East, a good part of the year was spent hunting buffalo that met their needs in so many ways.

Enormous herds of buffalo, numbering in the millions, moved north and south depending on the season. In summer Indians lived in teepees and followed the migration patterns of the buffalo. To facilitate hunting on the grassy prairies large tribes broke up into smaller family groups. Family ties were strong and there was a deep feeling of affection between members of a family. The whole tribe gathered again at the autumn festival where they celebrated their reunion by ceremonial dances, held their initiation rites, and made special offerings to the Sky Father. In winter they would return to their larger earth houses near the rivers and their gardens. From here they would journey out in search of deer, antelope, beaver, and fox.

The religious life of the hunting tribes of the Great Plains was not as well organized as the religious life of the more stable tribes of the east that gradually became involved in agriculture. The religious life of Plains Indians was centered on the all powerful and all seeing Sky Father who guarded the world and watched over its people. Between this omnipresent power and the earth which he protected there was a realm of eagles, thunder, lightning, the rainbow, the sun, and the moon. These lesser powers were intermediaries between the Sky Father and the Indians. They often intervened in Indian affairs. They inspired warriors; they directed the migration paths of the buffalo; they caused storms and floods or caused rivers to run dry. These spirits could be propitiated by offerings of human suffering or the self-inflicted wounds and pain as in the Sun Dance.

Since the Plains Indians led such a mobile existence there were few permanent shrines of any sort connected with their religious practices. In place of permanent shrines these Indians venerated a kind of portable shrine known as medicine bundles, which were carried with them on hunting expeditions or on excursions of war. These bundles contained the relics of ancient ancestors or sacred objects given the ancients by their gods to protect them and bring good fortune. These bundles were a kind of family or tribal property belonging to those to whom the gods had entrusted it. There were rites of song and dance and ritual customs connected with them. Many Indian myths developed around these sacred medicine bundles. There were special people appointed to be keepers of these bundles.

Zuni shield
Museum of the
American Indian
Heye Foundation
NY

MEDICINE BUNDLES MYTH

Medicine bundles issued from
    A tribes religious belief,
A kind of shrine that could be moved
    To ward off future grief.

The red man had no sacred place,
    For places were too fixed.
A transient life and stable shrines,
    They felt could not be mixed.

These bundles then were substitutes
    For shrines in other creeds.
They carried them on all their trips
    To meet religious needs.

They believed each bundle held within
    Gifts given by the gods,
That would protect the Indian
    On any path he trods.

Most tribes possessed these bundled shrines.
    Each bundle had a name.
The bundles were of different types,
    But evil overcame.

When there appeared a special need,
  In family or in tribe,
The sacred bundle was unwrapped
  To show what was inside.

In days of old when food was scarce,
  And buffalo departed,
The children cried from hunger pangs,
  Distressed and brokenhearted.

The women begged the chief to call
  The sacred bundle's keeper.
That bundle known as "Knot in Tree,"
  Might ward off death's Grim Reaper."

The chief first offered to the gods
  Tobacco's sacred smoke.
The bundle then was opened wide
  God's blessings to evoke.

A pole with gifts for all the gods,
  Before the teepee stood.
The people sat in silent awe,
  As priests sang chants they should.

These chants reminded buffalo
  Of promises they'd made,
That buffalo would meet man's need,
  When sacred bundle bade.

Three days these rites continued on,
  Till tribe began to wonder.
But then they heard the buffalo
  That pounded ground like thunder.

The priest then sent a brave young man
  To capture a young bull.
He brought it to the chief's teepee
  And laid it out in full.

The priest then told this ancient myth
  Of buffalo when man,
A myth in praise of buffalo,
  Who now would feed this clan.

In days of old all mankind lived
  In caves beneath the ground.
Above them roamed the buffalo,
  The world was their compound.

The priest spoke of those ancient days,
     When buffalo were bred.
They looked like men in every way,
     But had horns on their head.

They kept a sacred bundle called,
     "The Knot Up In The Tree."
When buffalo got hungry,
     They went there trustingly.

Four days they sang their magic chants,
     And struck four times the knot.
Though you think this incredible,
     Here's what their deeds begot.

Some humans beings underground
     Came from the tree they beat.
The buffalo then hunted them,
     Like animals to eat.

Their human victims were cut up,
     Stretched out on drying frame.
The buffalo then gaily danced,
     Before they ate their game.

But one young man escaped this fate,
    Outrunning his pursuers.
He hid among the tangled brush,
    From bison evildoers.

One day while he was hunting food,
    A girl walked by in haste.
Her head was horned; her leather white;
    Her hair hung to her waist.

He followed her to where she lived,
    And entered her teepee.
Then feeling safe, he soon dozed off,
    For he was very sleepy.

When he awoke she spoke to him.
    She told her people's plight.
She said all buffalo wished to be
    True animals outright.

The youth could bring that feat about,
    If he were brave enough.
He'd have to trick flesh-eating guards,
    Which she would help him bluff.

She led him past the warrior guards
    In buffalo disguise.
The guards thought they smelled human flesh,
    Then felt their thought unwise.

He snuck into the chieftain's tent
    And heard his chants of shame.
He saw the staff that struck the tree
    From which food people came.

He saw the racks of drying flesh,
    Of human hands and head.
As anger grew to boiling point,
    He said things best unsaid.

White Buffalo Woman said to him:
    "Make weapons we can hide.
We'll take them to the knotted tree,
    Then speak to those inside."

They hid these weapons under skins,
    Lest buffalo would see.
She then told men what they should do,
    When called to leave the tree.

You must grab bow and arrow, then,
    And shoot a Buffalo man.
So when the chief struck at the tree,
    Each followed her command.

As men departed from the tree,
    They shot a Buffalo man.
As each was hit, it then became
    A true buffalo, then ran.

It ran till it found prairie grass,
    Which then became its food.
No longer did it feed on men,
    But men now it pursued.

White Buffalo girl and boy were wed,
    And they begot a race.
The Arikara nation is
    The fruit of their embrace.

That sacred bundle, Knot In Tree,
    Is still that race's guide,
For they still eat the buffalo
    But not all that's inside.

They won't eat lumps on frontal legs.
    On that meat there's a ban,
For it could be ancestral flesh,
    When buffalo ate man.

Most think this fable is bizarre,
    A shaman gone berserk!
With dancing, drums, and sacred rites
    That guaranteed his work.

I think it's just that Indians
    All recognized a debt,
That men owe to the universe,
    Which they must not forget.

They knew all things were somehow one,
    But how, they did not know.
They knew their dead watched over them,
    But didn't know how-so.

They knew the chief creator god
    And lesser spirits, too,
Protected them in many ways
    In everything they do.

They knew of all their blessings,
    The buffalo was best.
Its food, its hide, its horns and hair,
    Stood far above the rest.

So it is any wonder then
    That beast was so extolled,
Or mysteries surrounded it,
    And fables multifold.

Zuni fetish
Private collection

CAUSALITY AND MYTH

Mythology is a culture's ancient account of the supernatural world. It seeks to reveal the origins and genealogy of the gods and spirits that govern the universe. Each race culture, or nation has its ancient beliefs which it seeks to communicate to future generations. Those efforts to communicate those beliefs are known as mythology. The development of a nation's mythology follows along its efforts to account for the world around them. Adults as well as children ask the question WHY, and questions demand answers. When answers are not obvious, they are thought out or concocted by wise men who are called upon by others to answer the question WHY.

Answers were handed down through word of mouth by story tellers and poets, by singers and bards. Myths were told and retold, with some additions along the way to extol or to boast. However, listeners knew them so well from repetition, that they would not tolerate anything that would mutilate the message or destroy its force.

Since mythology was basically concerned with the causality of things and events in the world around man, the stories and tales in which a mythology was framed was meant to instruct as well as to entertain.

Someone once said that myths and folklore "are as old as time and as new as tomorrow." I think this is very true and we shall see it demonstrated in the following causality tales according to Indian mythology.

Navajo sand painting--Shooting Way
Wheelwright Museum of the American Indian, Sante Fe

WHY BLUEBIRDS ARE BLUE
AND COYOTES ARE NOT

The bluebird was not always blue.
    Its color was quite ugly.
Nearby a lake it made a nest,
    Which held the bird quite snugly.

It bathed within the lake each day,
    Four times it bathed each morning.
And as it bathed it sang a song,
    Its ugly color scorning.

It praised the water's color blue,
    And made a silent wish.
It swam within the lake each day
    As if it were a fish.

It shed it feathers on day four,
    And left the lake bare-skinned.
It grew blue feathers on day five
    Which fluttered in the wind.

The bird was now a happy bird,
    So proud of being blue.
And people looked and sang its praise,
    As through the skies it flew.

When green coyote witnessed this
    Its jealousy then grew.
And when it heard the bluebird's praise,
    It wanted to be blue.

And so it sought the bluebird out,
    Which told it what to do.
And when coyote left the lake
    It was a brilliant blue.

Coyote then pranced all around
    To show off his new hue.
He sought his shadow in the sun
    To see if it were blue.

He strutted in his vanity,
    This foolish extrovert.
In pompous pride he hit a stump
    And fell into the dirt.

The blue coyote hit the dust,
    But really wasn't hurt.
And since that day coyotes are
    Described in shades of dirt.

Pride always comes before the fall.
    A fall will follow pride.
And that will always be the case,
    When meekness goes untried.

So if you walk in Satan's pride,
    You'll fall upon your face.
And as you do, you'll pick up dust,
    Not easy to erase.

Apache basket
Museum of the American Indian
Heye Foundation, NY

THE ORIGIN OF
THE HOPI SNAKE DANCE

There was a boy who did not believe
    In deities or gods.
He set out for their dwelling place
    Just to improve his odds.

He met the rain god on his trip,
    Tewa, the Silent One.
He wouldn't believe what Tewa said,
    Nor cease his trip begun.

Tewa assumed his godlike form,
    Much to the young boy's fright.
But he determined to go on,
    And soon was out of sight.

The angry cloud god then appeared,
    And scolded this young lad.
He, too, assumed his godlike form
    And further steps forbade.

The god said he could go unto
    The Village of the Snake.
But once there, he must go back home,
    And further steps forsake.

And as the boy proceeded on
  Star-Flicker god appeared.
He wore the feathers of great birds
  Which he had commandeered.

He, too, put limits on the boy:
  "Snake Village, but look out!
Its many snakes will try to bite
  Because you live in doubt."

The god then gave the boy an herb,
  To keep the snakes away.
He told the boy how he could reach
  The leader's house to stay.

Things happened as the god foretold.
  The herbs stopped each snake's bite.
The boy then found the leader's house
  And there he spent the night.

These snakes could change to human form
  And bid snake life adieu.
The leader and his daughters
  Looked like all humans do.

The leader told his visitor
    To leave or lose his life.
He gave the lad his daughter,
    Which he took as his wife.

The two were told: "Make piki bread,"
    To spread along the way,
In white and yellow, red and blue,
    Which turned to colored clay.

These colors were the gifts from snakes
    Which Hopi turned to paint.
To paint their pottery and skins,
    And moccasins quite quaint.

The wife grew large with child within,
    And sent her spouse ahead,
To reach his home and gather food,
    But first this warning said.

"Touch no one on your journey home,
    And let no one touch you.
Until you have returned to me,
    The things I've asked, please do."

So he went home to family
    And rapped with them all night.
He spoke of wife and coming child
    In words of great delight.

Next morning he then gathered food
    And to his wife he raced.
A former lover on the path
    Ran up and him embraced.

His wife already knew of this
    When he arrived with food.
She said: "You do not love me.
    Of this I've certitude."

She wept and said, "Now I must leave.
    My life with you is done.
I shall return to my snake life,
    But first I'll bear your son."

She bore a son who could, at will,
    Change self into a snake.
And still today the Hopi dance
    The snake dance for his sake.

The Hopi are descendants of
    This son of brave and snake.
And as they dance with snakes in mouth
    Their past they reawake.

I'm sure they're lessons we can learn,
    From this myth, though it's strange.
First, don't put rattlers in your mouth,
    Unless you are deranged.

And surely do not marry one,
    As did this Hopi brave,
Whose troubles started as a boy,
    When he did not behave.

The poor lad first denied the gods,
    Then laughed at their commands.
And that is why throughout this myth,
    He suffered at their hands.

And this will be the fate of all,
    Who in their foolish pride.
Will disregard what they have learned
    And put their past aside.

For when the sacred's put aside,
    Each man is his own law.
He thinks that when he speaks his mind
    All others stand in awe.

He rides roughshod upon weak men
    Who tolerate abuse.
But men who fight for principles
    One day will cook his goose.

I'm sure this myth taught Indians
    A reverence for their past,
And kept traditions that they loved
    From the iconoclast.

It's too bad that all liturgists
    Can't learn these lessons taught.
Then possibly they could undo
    The harm that they have wrought.

Anasazi art
Museum of Indian Art and Culture, Santa Fe

WHY MOLES LIVE UNDERGROUND

The mole now lives beneath the ground,
  But not in former days.
It used to roam the countryside
  And loved the sun's bright rays.

When moles were insignificant,
  They walked above the earth.
No one would try to capture them
  For they had little worth.

But then a mole upstaged the wise,
  At least that's what I've heard.
It did what shamans could not do,
  And then was sepulchred.

The reason why moles met this fate
  Was due to one's compassion.
It seems it did for a young brave
  What shamans could not fashion.

That brave had fallen deep in love,
  But love was not returned.
Each time he sought the maiden's hand,
  His love was always spurned.

The brave then sought a shaman's help
   And told him of his plight.
The shaman said that he could help.
   And she'd be his that night.

Contrariwise, her fury grew.
   She loved less than before.
Although the shaman cast his spells,
   The maiden loathed him more.

The brave was sad and deeply hurt,
   He couldn't sleep or eat.
Discouraged, roaming in despair,
   A mole he chanced to meet.

The mole declared it could relieve
   The sadness in his life.
It said the maiden soon would come
   And ask to be his wife.

That night the mole bore underground
   Into the maiden's tent.
And while she slept it took her heart,
   And then it quickly went.

It brought her heart back to the brave,
"Now swallow this," it said.
The young brave did as he was told,
But thought his lover dead.

But she was very much alive,
And now was much in love.
She wanted what she once disdained.
The hawk became a dove.

The lovely maiden was confused,
When she loved whom she hated.
The clod she once thought very dull,
She presently now rated.

As flames of love burned deep within,
She asked to be his bride.
All this was done because the brave
Possessed her heart inside.

Quite soon these two young Indians
Were known as man and wife.
And that's when moles were forced to live
A subterranean life.

The shaman flew into a rage,
  Upstaged by this small mole.
And so to flee the shaman's scourge
  It burrowed in a hole.

When moles were insignificant,
  They led a life quite free.
But once they threatened shamans' fraud.
  Such freedom could not be.

For when a man is insecure,
  He persecutes his threat.
It was that way when moles were free,
  And it is that way yet.

The world is filled with shaman-types,
  We see them all around.
They prance and parade and give advice
  That seldom is profound.

They sit in courts and serve on boards
  Where they do not belong.
They're always giving counsel,
  Which usually is wrong.

They're where they are for what they'll do,
    And not for what they know.
They'll be "yes men" to party lines
    And principles forego.

Because they're weak they cannot stand
    The voice of opposition.
They'll first ignore and then condemn,
    And hold an Inquisition.

Their narrow minds will force weak foes
    To flee beneath the ground.
And then they'll boast that all agree
    And think their judgment sound.

The wise must not be cowardly moles.
    They must not hide, but fight.
They must not bend to bigotry,
    But fight for what is right.

Mimbres pottery art
Maxwell Museum of Anthropology
University of Mexico, Albuquerque

THE ORIGIN OF THE FLUTE

The only songs a flute should play
   Are songs that speak of love.
And those who know its history,
   Know what I'm speaking of.

There was a time when Indians
   Had only drums and rattles.
And these they beat or shook with force
   When they engaged in battles.

But when it came to sounds of love
   They had no instrument.
They had no sounds to emphasize,
   Just what their love words meant.

This sound of love was found within
   The sweet sound of the flute,
That once a young brave chanced upon
   And which he learned to toot.

The tale of this discovery
   I now shall tell to you.
And if you've heard it told before,
   This can be a review.

A lot of winters, long ago,
   A brave was hunting game.
That brave is rather famous now,
   Though no one knows his name.

He chased an elk into the woods
   But there he lost his quest.
He ate the food he brought along,
   And then laid down to rest.

In forests there are many sounds
   From animals to owl,
From rustling branches in the breeze,
   To night-things on the prowl.

The brave now heard a doleful sound,
   He'd never heard before.
At first afraid, he grasped his bow,
   His courage to restore.

But soon the sound was like a song,
   So sad, but full of hope,
Portraying love and love's desires,
   With which each man must cope.

The brave then slept and dreamed about
    A woodpecker in flight.
It called to him, "Come follow me."
    Brave followed by moonlight.

The sun was high when he awoke,
    And on a branch he saw
The red woodpecker calling him,
    By waving with its claw.

It flew from one tree to the next,
    But looking back to see,
If this young brave were following
    To find the magic key.

The bird flew to a cedar tree
    And hammered till midnoon.
And when the wind began to blow,
    There came that mournful tune.

The gust of wind had whistled through
    The holes the bird had drilled.
And with the sound of harmony
    The forest air was filled.

The Wisdom of American Indian Mythology

He took the hollow branch of wood,
　　Replete with little holes,
Back to his home so he could bring
　　This joy to other souls.

He blew on it, but no sound came.
　　The Indian was sad.
He fasted then for four long days,
　　And then a vision had.

The bird once more flew back to him,
　　Appearing as a man.
Then in a dream revealed to him
　　How he could pipe like Pan.

The flute must be of cedar wood,
　　And shaped much like a bird,
With longish neck and opened mouth,
　　To make the sounds he'd heard.

From hole to hole his hand must move,
　　Just like that man in dreams.
And when it's done in just that way,
　　Sweet music flows in streams.

In music, love is best expressed,
    Especially by the flute.
And this the hunter verified,
    When he began to toot.

The daughter of the village chief,
    Found no man good enough.
And when men called for courting her,
    They soon would be rebuffed.

But she was whom the hunter sought,
    No other bride would do.
So he composed a special song
    Which on his flute he blew.

And when chief's daughter heard its strains,
    She could not stop her feet.
They ran to him so rapidly,
    Some thought it indiscreet.

And since that day when lovers met,
    The flute's been man's ally.
For even though they're warrior braves,
    All Indians are shy.

The Wisdom of American Indian Mythology

Since they can't say what's in their hearts,
    They speak in courting song.
They are too shy to speak with words
    To those for whom they long.

When braves meet "winchinchalas,"
    The girls whom they adore,
They let their flutes speak of their love
    In words girls can't ignore.

For when girls hear that plaintive sound
    Of "siyotanka" flutes,
They know it is a call to them,
    Unless they are deaf mutes.

So every man who's shy today
    Will have some kind of flute.
And it will be for him, at least,
    A kind of substitute.

A man will speak more bravely when
    A proxy mouths his words.
But for this fine procedure,
    He has to thank the birds.

As birds taught man to toot the flute
    And moles to excavate,
So nature lays out many things
    That we should imitate.

And if we follow nature's path,
    Our steps will never fail.
But moccasins must find the tracks,
    For there's no other trail.

So follow very carefully
    Where paths of nature lead.
And walk upon them faithfully
    So that you will succeed.

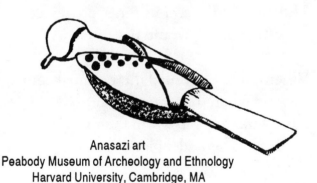

Anasazi art
Peabody Museum of Archeology and Ethnology
Harvard University, Cambridge, MA

HOW THE PINES CAME
TO SHARE THEIR FIRE

Before mankind lived on the earth,
 The trees and beasts were friends.
They walked together sharing things,
 Which paid great dividends.

But only pines could make a fire,
 Through secrets never told.
Thus only pines could warm themselves,
 Whenever it got cold.

One time when bitter winter came,
 The animals all froze.
They sought the secrets pines possessed,
 Which pines would not disclose.

When pines convened their annual court,
 And when that court began,
Pines built a fire to warm themselves,
 But beaver had a plan.

This conclave was in Idaho,
 Along Grande Ronde River.
Pines posted guards along the bank
 With arrows in their quiver.

The beaver hid along the shore,
    Just waiting for a chance.
He'd have to do things carefully,
    Or he would catch a lance.

A burning coal rolled down the bank,
    An offshoot of their fire.
The beaver hid it in his breast
    Which made his skin perspire.

The beaver then sped down the stream,
    With pines in hot pursuit.
They made a rather funny sight,
    As they were seen enroute.

The pines continued chasing him
    To scourge him for his deed.
But they grew tired and took their rest
    Before they could proceed.

It's there that you will find them still,
    For they grew very tired.
A few of them continued on
    But then they soon expired.

They're scattered now at intervals,
Along the river's bank.
It seems they still are searching for
The one who pulled that prank.

The last pine in that river chase
Saw beaver give their flame
To willows, birch, and other trees,
That still don't have a name.

To any tree that wanted fire
The beaver gladly gave it.
And they in turn will give their flame
To all those men who crave it.

They'll give their fire when rubbed just right.
Just like the ancient pine.
Then suddenly a flame appears,
And smoke will be its sign.

Today man does not understand
The truth behind these myths.
He strikes a match or turns a knob
And fire comes forthwith.

But man must learn to comprehend,
    The hardships of the past.
Unless he learns them thoroughly
    Their values will not last.

For nothing comes now easily,
    That one time was not toil.
The things we take for granted now
    Once caused men great turmoil.

So let us all appreciate,
    The things forefathers gave.
The fire we now have instantly
    Sent beavers to their grave.

Navajo sand painting--Earth
Wheelwright Museum of the American Indian, Santa Fe

THE ORIGIN OF MOSQUITOES

An evil giant lived on earth,
  Who loved to eat man's flesh.
He ate man's heart and drank man's blood,
  And loved it best when fresh.

The Indians were terrified,
  As neighbors disappeared.
One brave then said he'd kill the fiend,
  And all his tribesmen cheered.

He placed himself upon a path
  Pretending to be dead,
Then waited for the giant's bulk,
  That soon stood overhead.

The ugly giant took him home
  To feed his appetite.
But first he needed firewood
  To cook him with that night.

He threw the brave upon the floor
  And went in search of wood.
The brave grabbed the giant's knife
  With all the strength he could.

The brave then saw the giant's son,
    And put knife to his throat.
"Where does your father's heart reside?
    Tell me, or thee I'll smote."

"His heart is in his left foot's heel!"
    The giant's son cried out.
"But what good will that knowledge do?
    Soon you'll be inside out."

The giant's feet were at the door.
    The left foot first came through.
The brave then thrust the knife in it
    And cut his heart in two.

The giant died and fell to earth,
    But still his voice could speak:
"I'll keep on eating human flesh;
    Your blood I'll always seek."

To make sure giant's words were lies,
    The brave cut him to pieces.
He threw those bits on the fire,
    With hope the voice decreases.

When brave threw ashes to the wind,
    Mosquitoes came to be.
Their numbers were unlimited,
    As far as eyes could see.

The giant's voice was heard once more:
    "I'll eat all human flesh.
I'll siphon off your tasty blood.
    And drink it when it's fresh."

And as he spoke, man felt a sting.
    Mosquitoes took their bite.
When man began to scratch himself,
    The bugs took off in flight.

So often times we see in life,
    One thing leads to the next.
One problem solved, another comes.
    This makes us quite perplexed.

But we must take them one by one.
    And take each one in turn.
To try to solve them all at once,
    Is surely to get burned.

So do not be discouraged when
    Life's problems come your way.
There'll always be tomorrow,
    Which is another day.

The problems that are here today,
    I'm sure will leave tomorrow.
But then there'll come some other ones,
    That might bring you more sorrow.

So line up all life's problems then,
    And take them each in stride.
For all of life's mosquitoes,
    There's some insecticide.

Mimbres pottery design
Museum of the American Indian, Heye Foundation, NY

WHY BUTTERFLIES ARE SILENT

One day the Chief Creator sat
    And watched the children play.
But soon his heart grew very sad,
    At least that's what they say.

He thought of children's future life,
    And what that life would hold,
Their graying hair and wrinkled skin,
    And missing teeth when old.

These pretty girls would all grow fat.
    The hunter's arm would fail.
One day old men would all go blind,
    And fresh love would grow stale.

The beauty of the trees and flowers
    Would wither and would fade.
The warrior filled with bravery now,
    One day would be afraid.

Creator's heart grew heavier
    With thoughts of coming winter,
When leaves would turn and fall to earth,
    And buffalo grow thinner.

But now the yellow sun was bright,
    The sky a brilliant blue.
The leaves were green and yellowish,
    And white was each canoe.

A glint then came into His eye,
    And joy came to His heart.
Such colors had to be preserved
    In living works of art.

The blackness of the children's hair.
    The yellow of the sun,
The red and blue of flowers,
    The tint of cinnamon.

He gathered all these colors in
    From everything on earth.
He put them all into a bag,
    Then made the bag give birth.

But first he threw into the bag,
    The lovely songs of birds.
So when he made the butterflies,
    The song of birds was heard.

These butterflies flew overhead
　　And danced about in flight.
These children never once had seen
　　A more attractive sight.

And when those butterflies sang songs,
　　The children listened, smiling.
But then the birds came to complain,
　　Their angry gripes compiling.

They scolded the Creator god,
　　And said it wasn't right,
That he would give those songs away,
　　That birds sang in their flight.

They said that he had promised birds,
　　That each would have its song.
To share that gift with others then
　　To them somehow seemed wrong.

Creator readily agreed
　　And took from butterflies
The lovely gift of singing songs,
　　As they flew through the skies.

This story somehow speaks to us,
  As myths were meant to do.
There's something here for each of us,
  As if this myth were true.

Though each of us has certain gifts,
  There are some gifts we lack.
And if we have more than our share,
  We ought to give some back.

But this should never make us sad.
  Our loss is someone's gain.
And if it brings him happiness,
  Then why should we complain.

We should enjoy what others have.
  Variety means life.
The opposite is selfishness,
  And selfishness means strife.

Rejoice that things are as they are.
  Diversity is great.
Be satisfied with what you have,
  Before it is too late.

For God might give to butterflies
　　The things you treasure most.
He'll always take His gifts from you,
　　If you begin to boast.

So gather all the colors of
　　The world in which you live.
And if you have more than your share,
　　Don't be afraid to give.

And gather all the songs you sing,
　　And share them all with joy.
The things you give come back to build;
　　But things you keep destroy.

Yes, there are lessons in each myth,
　　Which call us all to terms.
If we are selfish like the birds,
　　We'll end up eating worms.

Zuni mask
Private collection

WHY CROWS ARE BLACK

There was a time when crows were white
    When earth was very young,
And buffalo roamed everywhere,
    As we know from their dung.

All hunting then was done on foot.
    The horse had not arrived;
Nor had the red men booming guns,
    By which white men survived.

And so it was quite difficult
    To bring these great beasts down.
That's why the thought of sly white crows,
    Caused Indians to frown.

The crows were friends of buffalo.
    And soared up in the sky.
They warned them of the hunter's search,
    And served them as a spy.

The red men held a council then
    To see what they should do.
They said they'd have to teach white crows
    A bitter thing or two.

The problem was to capture one,
  Before an ally warns.
A brave then dressed in buffalo skin,
  Which still had head and horns.

He roamed among the buffalo,
  As if he were but grazing.
He looked just like those awesome beasts,
  Which truly were amazing.

As hunters marched out from their camp,
  The crows cried out their warning.
The buffalo all galloped off
  Into the dusty morning.

But one remained, the brave disguised,
  Pretending not to hear.
The chief crow landed on his back
  To tell him death was near.

The brave reached up and grabbed its leg
  The crow could not escape.
I guess that crow was "buffaloed"
  By what was in skin's cape.

They tied it with a rawhide string.
　　A powwow then was called.
When sentenced to burn at the stake
　　The white crow was appalled.

But council fires burned through the string.
　　The crow then flew away.
But it was singed and badly charred,
　　So it is black today.

It wondered why those buffalo,
　　Did not come to its aid.
They could stampede and counteract
　　That buffalo charade.

The crows said they'd not help again
　　Those ungrateful buffaloes.
For it was due to their neglect
　　That white became black crows.

Ingratitude's an ugly thing,
　　Which always will forget
The things that others shared with us,
　　Their life and calumet.

There is in every one of us
   A little of that vice.
That we should seek to cast it out
   Is surely sound advice.

For it will always alienate,
   The very ones we love.
The ingrate wears exclusion,
   Which fits him like a glove.

Appreciate the things you have,
   Especially what is given.
If you are grateful, you will find
   All other faults forgiven.

San Ildefonso pottery design
Museum of Indian Art and Culture, Santa Fe

ANCIENT BELIEFS TODAY

Indians of old were wise enough to know that all things must have a cause, and they were honest enough to face the demands of that conclusion. The reader today, then, is not surprised to see that ancient Indians inquired into the origin of everything from the mosquito to the flute, or that Indians always sought the ultimate reason for any happening, such as why crows were black, why moles lived beneath the ground, and why butterflies were silent. All this was a part of the Indian's native intellectual curiosity, and so it is to be expected that it was also a part of the Indians' mythology and folklore.

Although few Indian tribes today have retained their ancient tribal organizations, many individual Indians still revere and hold sacred the customs and traditions of their ancestors.

The ancient Indian mythology, in which man offered his prayers and his sufferings to the gods and brought those gods into a special relationship with his tribal community by the reenactment or recitation of the myth, is, for the most part, now treated as mere folk tale by modern Indians. Ancient ceremonies are placed in a more contemporary setting today. Ancient chants are still sung and religious dances and rituals still performed, but mostly on reservations for the benefit of tourists. This practice is not superstitious. One can certainly reverence the religious beliefs of one's ancestors without making those beliefs one's own.

Their ancient mythology and their venerable customs derived from it are clear echoes of Indian past history and religious beliefs. It would be tragic, however, if that almost inaudible echo were ever silenced or destroyed by disinterest on the part of Indians or by antagonism on the part of modern civilization. The passing of time and changes in lifestyles will always cause the memory of the past to fade. This is unfortunate. It is to counteract this situation that the traditions of a people or a nation, which have so influenced their past, must be diligently preserved in the present and continued, at least culturally and artistically, in the future.

Among the Indians, myths were often linked to healing ceremonies. This is a major reason why these ancient myths were committed to memory and preserved in ritual by shamans and tribal leaders. Both those who witnessed the reenactment of the myth and those who performed that reenactment felt they were in some way integrated more deeply into the world of the spirit and the world of nature.

They felt then that things were as they should be. In this way the religious chants and ceremonial dances served as a kind of psychotherapy which aided the personal or social integration between the gods and men. All the important events in tribal life were used in some way to relate man to the gods. People depended daily on the blessing of the gods for success in hunting or farming, and, to some extent, the gods depended on peoples' prayers and rituals to be recognized.

Navajo sand painting--Red Ant Chant
Wheelwright Museum of the American Indian, Santa Fe

THE TRICKSTER HERO

The Indian was wise, indeed,
    And knew all things were caused.
But when it came to certain things,
    The red man often paused.

When explanations were in doubt,
    He called the Trickster-Hero.
He summoned "Saynday" to explain
    When causes known were zero.

Saynday was known in ancient myths
    Of how things came to be.
He also was the hidden cause
    Of each catastrophe.

He's seen as a coyote,
    In many red man stories.
But sometimes he's a raven, though,
    In some myths' inventories.

Each tribe gave him a different name,
    But one thing was quite clear.
When things were quite abnormal,
    They knew that he was near.

Some say the five bright Pleiad stars
    Are but his fingerprints.
To show that he's still watching us,
    He gives us starlike hints.

One day this Saynday visited
    The village of the dogs.
The dogs were talking all at once,
    In noisy dialogues.

The Trickster asked them to be still:
    "Please, hush, so I can speak."
But every dog and puppy's voice
    Then reached a higher peak.

Again the Trickster yelled, "Shut up.
    Please stop that noise, I say.
And if you don't, I'll punish you
    And I will start today."

But dogs talked louder than before,
    And Trickster was upset.
He took the power of speech from them,
    And none of them speaks yet.

Dogs still can yap and growl and bark,
    But that's of no avail.
The only way that dogs can talk
    Is with their eyes and tail.

When dogs converse with people now,
    It's only in this way.
With smiling eyes and wagging tail,
    They say what they must say.

So discourse of your family dog
    Must be with tail and eye.
That's why dogs are such faithful pets,
    For tails and eyes can't lie.

Your dog is there to welcome you
    With love as tail does wag.
And though it's late when you get home,
    Its eyes will never nag.

Dogs' tails tell you they're still your friend,
    When other friends betray.
And if you read their loving eyes,
    You know that's what they say.

In time all dogs learned to obey.
    When man commands, they listen.
It's too bad past dogs did not heed
    The Trickster's admonition!

For if they did, and still could speak,
    Who knows what dogs would say?
Would they deceive us with their words
    And faithlessness portray?

If so, we are quite fortunate
    That dogs speak with their tails.
For as they wag in loyalty,
    We know friendship prevails.

Mimbres pottery art
Maxwell Museum of Anthropology
University of New Mexico, Albuquerque

HOW HEALING BEGAN

At first God made the universe.
    He then created man.
He gave each man a piece of earth
    According to His plan.

The Indians lived in one spot,
    But were unhappy there.
So God then let them spread about
    And move their homes elsewhere.

The red men found great happiness
    In their new bailiwick.
There Indians were quite content
    Till two of them got sick.

No one had heard of illnesses,
    Nor knew about a cure.
Why sick got sicker every day,
    No one was really sure.

Then He who made the universe
    Addressed those who were well.
He told them they should cure the sick
    And their disease dispel.

"There is a cure for every ill
    And every kind of sickness.
And if your prayers and songs are right,
    The cure will come with quickness."

So God gave man the knowledge of
    What songs and chants to sing.
If they were sung as God prescribed,
    Health would return full-swing.

And this is just what happened.
    The sick regained their health.
And since that day our prayers became,
    More valuable than wealth.

This is the ancient origin
    Of curing ceremonies,
Which have survived unto this day,
    In spite of many phonies.

If there were red men lawyers then,
    Malpractice prayers would be.
I'm sure, if health were not restored,
    Those lawyers got their fee.

And man today still prays for things,
  In prayer and song and chant.
And we are very confident,
  What man seeks God will grant.

We see that myth is based on life
  Which man finds incomplete.
Unless man understands this fact,
  His life is self-deceit.

Ceremonial loincloth

Ceremonial sash

Ceremonial wand

Silver pin

Tray

Hopi art
Peabody Museum of Archeology and Ethnology
Harvard University, Cambridge, MA

DANCING TO THE SUN

The Tsis-tsistas Indians danced to the sun from time immemorial. The sun dance was gradually adopted by many tribes among the Plains Indians. This sun dance represented the making of the universe by Maheo, the Creator, and his helper, Great Roaring Thunder. It represented the making of the sun, moon, stars, and universe. It was the most sacred of all Indian ceremonies.

Long ago when the earth was young, the Cheyenne were starving. No rain had fallen in many months. The animals of the forests were dying. The Cheyenne had only their dogs to eat. It was at this time that they left their native lands in search of food.

The old chief then saw how thin his people had become. He had a vision that all men should go to the woman he felt most attracted to and beg her to give him something to eat. A young warrior, attracted to the beautiful wife of the chief, went to her. She fed him dog soup. The warrior then told her that she should go north with him, for it had fallen on him to save his people. The young warrior told the chief's wife that Maheo, the Creator, had informed him in a vision that she should accompany him to a medicine lodge in the north. This lodge was Maheo's symbol of the universe. There Maheo would instruct them in a sacred ritual which they then were to teach the Cheyenne. If the Cheyenne performed this sacred rite, rains would fall, plants would grow green, and buffalo would be plentiful.

The beautiful woman went north with him. Each night she set up their teepee to face the sun. They came to a lake and entered a great mountain through a rock and found themselves in a medicine lodge. Here Maheo and Roaring Thunder instructed them for four days. They were told that the sun, moon, stars, and universe would move in harmony, rains would fall, corn and chokecherries would ripen, wild turnips and herbs would be plentiful, and herds of buffalo and antelope would come, whenever the sun dance was performed. They were to wear "issiwun," the sacred hat, when this hallowed and religious dance to the sun was performed.

As the young warrior, now medicine man, and the chief's wife left the mountain, streams of buffalo left with them. Herbs and plants grew all around them. They were clad in sacred dress and wore the sacred hat. At the end of the day they rested, as did the animals following them. They made love each evening and sang the song Maheo had taught them. They returned to the village and told the people all that Maheo had taught them. This was the origin of the Cheyenne Sun Dance.

The Cheyenne then built a medicine lodge, as the young warrior had instructed them. They painted their bodies in a sacred manner and sang the prescribed songs. Children fashioned clay figures of animals as symbols of life's renewal. When these clay animals were placed in the lodge, real animals grazed nearby. Thereafter the young warrior was named "Horns Standing Up," because the prescribed sacred hat had two horns.

The sun dance took place once a year, at the height of the summer. Other tribes soon adopted this religious ceremony and it immediately became the most awe-inspiring of all Indian ritual. The Ponca called it the "mystery dance," the Mandans called it the "okapi ceremony." In some tribes, such as the Sioux, the sun dance ceremony involved the *piercing* of the dancers. Sharp skewers were passed through their flesh as a form of self-torture. This is still done in Sioux sun dances today. In some tribes the self-torture involved fasting. The self-inflicted torture was offered as a sacrifice to the sun that others might live, that a sick friend recover from an illness, or that a son return from the warpath uninjured.

The sun dance is still performed among the Plains tribes. Although it was once outlawed by the U.S. government, it has now undergone a resurgence. The sun dance lodge is a circular building forty feet wide. It is walled and roofed with thatch boughs. The roof is supported by a cottonwood trunk. These are the dimensions alleged to have been given by Maheo to the young warrior so many years ago.

Kachina dolls
Private collection

THE SUN DANCE

No rain had fallen on the ground,
    The crops did not bear fruit.
The buffalo had disappeared,
    And men were destitute.

The earth itself was starving,
    As plants and trees all withered.
The hunters' game had all dropped dead,
    Though arrows still were quivered.

The Cheyenne tribes then left their homes
    In search for food and game.
They headed north and journeyed far,
    But found things just the same.

The chiefs looked at their starving tribes
    And fell into a vision.
And when they woke up from their trance,
    They issued this decision.

Each man must go and beg for food,
    From woman most admired,
From that one he's attracted to,
    The woman most desired.

A warrior asked the head chief's wife,
    For dog soup to imbibe.
He then told her that they were called
    To save the Cheyenne tribe.

He said that she must go with him,
    To some great distant land.
The spirit world conversed with him,
    And issued that command.

They pitched their teepee every night
    To face the rising sun.
And every morning they set out,
    Until their work was done.

They came to a great mountain where
    A rock revealed a door.
They crept inside the mountain then
    To see what was in store.

A spirit god was standing there
    Maheo, our creator.
He spoke a long time to his guests,
    Just like their educator.

He taught them both a sacred rite,
    A dance to bring forth rain.
And if they did it as prescribed,
    Great blessings they'd attain!

Great Roaring Thunder also spoke
    Throughout those four long days.
Instructing them in many things
    About their future ways.

Maheo told them to go home
    To teach the things they learned.
Great blessings would come to their tribe
    Once these vanguards returned.

"The sun and moon will fall in line.
    The stars will find accord.
The healing herbs will grow once more,
    And game will be restored."

"The buffalo and antelope
    Will roam the plains again.
And things will be as they should be
    For all the brave Cheyenne."

"The rains will fall to earth again
　　As will the gentle snow.
Once heaven is well-ordered
　　All things on earth will grow."

"But you must wear this sacred hat
　　Made from a bison's head.
Then Mother Earth will smile on you
　　And red men will be fed."

He placed the hat upon their heads,
　　And then the two departed.
A thundering herd of buffalo
　　Then followed as they started.

And as they walked plants sprouted up.
　　A gentle rain was falling.
The buffalo and antelope
　　Approached without them calling.

They sang the songs Maheo taught
　　Then headed for their home,
Somewhere beneath the western skies,
　　Where deer and bison roam.

The Wisdom of American Indian Mythology

When they arrived they taught their tribe
    The things the god besought.
They built a lodge and since have done
    The things Maheo taught.

So at the height of summertime
    Within their sun dance tent,
These tribes sing songs and do their dance,
    Till all their strength is spent.

The children place inside this lodge
    Clay animals they've made,
So that when braves called real beasts,
    The real ones obeyed.

And since that time so long ago
    Most tribes perform this dance.
With painted bodies songs are sung,
    Until they're in a trance.

This ancient myth then teaches us
    To what depths man will stoop,
If he gets ravenous enough
    To lunch upon dog soup.

This could have been the origin
    Of jitterbug or trot.
As men danced to the songs they sang,
    As if they were on "pot."

They proudly wore, as if a hat,
    A buffalo's fine head.
And then they pierced their bodies,
    Until their bodies bled.

They thought this would bring harmony
    To all the universe.
They thought that their shenanigans
    Would drive away god's curse.

And superstitions still are found
    In man's beliefs today.
As some reach out for rattlesnakes,
    And face their judgment day.

Some put themselves into a trance
    And speak with funny tongue.
They chatter incoherently
    As they become unstrung.

When reason is removed from faith,
  The crazies soon take over.
And though their sane world falls apart,
  They think they are in clover.

The miracles that happened once,
  Could happen yet again.
But I think God will first rely
  Upon the brains of men.

He made man master of this world
  To order and direct it.
So why should God then intervene,
  Whenever men neglect it?

I'm sure that God will hear our prayers,
  As He said He would do,
But in a way much differently
  Than we would like Him to.

Emotions sometimes follow thought,
  But they should never lead it.
And if they try, they'll not succeed.
  They only will impede it.

We see this in the Cheyenne's prayer
  Which put them in a trance.
But their emotions followed thought
  Which somehow made them dance.

Maheo ordered that they dance
  In honor of the sun.
To bring the planets into line
  And make all things be one.

Maheo heard the Cheyenne's prayer
  And sent them gentle rains.
The buffalo again appeared
  And roamed about the plains.

The universe was well again,
  And things began to grow.
And red men knew their prayers and dance
  Brought back the buffalo.

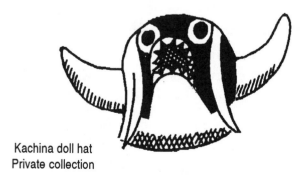

Kachina doll hat
Private collection

INDIANIZATION OF WHITES

European colonists felt certain that what wasn't European, wasn't civilized. To the European mind Indians seemed to lack both order and industry as well as continental manners. Their manners were considered brutish and barbarian. Indians seemed addicted to idleness. Polygamy was practiced in many tribes and divorce was but a matter of decision. Most tribes seemed to have no roots in the soil. Their homes were portable to fit their hunting habits. Indians felt they ought "by right of birth to enjoy the liberty of wild ass colts, rending no homage to anyone whomsoever, except when they liked."

Europeans who placed their priorities on fine clothing could not understand the Indian attitude that preferred to go naked. Fitted trousers were particularly abhorrent to Indian men who squatted to urinate. Europeans figured that an Indian could be civilized only when he suppressed his independence and native habits and dressed and acted like his European conquerors.

Again the reader is reminded not to generalize about Indians. Indians were of many different tribes and many cultural backgrounds. Some tribes were more advanced than others. Some were more concerned with agriculture than with hunting. Some lived in log houses rather than teepees. Some had constitutional forms of government, some were peaceful and kind while others were warlike and cruel.

In the beginning, Indians were very generous, hospitable, and even accommodating toward the English. But when two cultures meet there can be conflicts as well as cooperation. The more settlers advanced into Indian territory, destroyed the Indian's buffalo and confiscated his lands, the more constant became the threat and fear of war among colonists. On a strange frontier in a strange land, fear of Indian raids was magnified, especially among women. Indians were considered blood thirsty fiends who defiled any woman they took alive before putting her to death. Such fears were totally contrary to the testimony of those captured. There is no historical evidence at all that any white woman captured by Indians was raped. Indians had no sexual interest in white women. White women were unattractive to Indian men. Black was the color considered beautiful.

There were prisoners of war on both sides. Indians were captured by Europeans and Europeans were captured by Indians. As Europeans sought to Anglicize and Christianize their Indian captives, Indians sought to Indianize their European captives.

It is a fact of history that thousands of Europeans became Indians. Few Indians became Europeans. In 1782, it was reported that 21%-71% of the English captives refused to return to the English when ransomed. At that time three reasons were given for their refusal:

1. The Indian life was thought morally superior.
2. Captives were adopted as brothers and sisters.
3. Captives enjoyed their newly found freedom.

In 1753, Benjamin Franklin wrote:

"When an Indian child has been brought up among us, taught our language, and habituated to our customs, yet if he goes to see his relations and makes one Indian ramble with them, there is no persuading him ever to return. But when white children of either sex have been taken prisoners by the Indians and lived a while among them, then ransomed by their friends and treated with all imaginable tenderness to prevail on them to stay among the English, yet in a short time they become disgusted with our life and the care and pains that are necessary to support it, and take the first good opportunity of escaping again into the woods from whence there is no reclaiming them."

The Indian life, free of the cares and labors that are necessary to support the white man's manner of life with its infinite artificial wants, was appealing to captured Europeans. The openness and wilderness of the forest offered them more freedom than the intricate complexity of their own Puritan philosophy, with its burdens of civility and unlimited constraints. These "white" Indians fully accepted the Indian way of life, and often times they refused release when offered. If freedom were forced upon them, they regarded their deliverance as captivity and many ran away and fled back to their Indian homes and the adopted family they had grown to love. In those cases where whites did return to their own people, both they and the Indians wept bitterly at their departure.

The reason Indians took captives was to add to the membership of their own family and clan that had been depleted by tribal wars. Indians had a strong taboo against incest, and captive women were their future sisters and cousins. To defile them would be a serious disgrace to any Indian. Rape was the only capital crime punishable by the tribe. Even murder was not punished by the tribe but by the family of the one murdered. The fact that sexual abstinence was prescribed for three days before and after battle is a further argument against the rape of captured women. To offend their god in such a way would be to invite one's own death in battle.

Indians were especially kind to women and children captives. Even the beatings of male captives was more ceremonial than brutal. It was an initiation rite into Indian society, a purgation of white sins. It was a process whereby Indians could exorcise their anger and whites could begin their cultural transformation. Captives were washed in the river to purge out their whiteness. Their dress was changed to Indian dress, feathers, jewelry, and paint to signify they were now flesh of Indian flesh and bone of Indian bone. Once they were washed in the river in the adoption ceremony and the whiteness was washed away, Indians had an obligation to them to love, support, and defend them, for now there was no distinction between white and Indian. Whites even became chiefs. Captives soon learned to think, act, and react like Indians. This was the final step of Indianization. Children completed the process rather quickly and they speedily learned the new language.

To say that children became Indians because of the malleability of youth ignores the fact that Indian children did not become Europeans. Also, thousands of European adult captives stayed among

Indians even when they could have returned to their own families. According to their own testimony they stayed because Indian life appealed to them. They found in that life a strong sense of community, abundant love, and an uncommon integrity, values that the English honored but lived less successfully.

Indian mythology often speaks of white men in very derogatory terms. These ancient myths obviously followed unfortunate experiences that Indians had with white soldiers or settlers. The myths were not created before that experience, but following it. The perfidy, treachery, and deceit that marked and even characterized the white man's treatment of Indian tribes and individuals, especially in official treaties, is clearly articulated in Indian mythology. Indians looked upon the white man as "the bad guy," and for very good reasons. The word that best describes our country's official treatment of Native Americans during the periods of exploration, colonization, and settlement is a word "shameful," used in its worse sense.

Hopi design for
women's shawls
Private collection

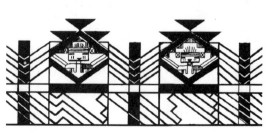

THE WHITE MAN IN MYTH

In ancient myths young Indians
    First learned about the whites.
But pictures that these myths portrayed
    Were not attractive sights.

Great Spirit made the world for man,
    Then placed man in the north.
There were no winters, ice, nor snow,
    But only spring, of course.

There animals of every sort,
    And fish and insects, too,
Could speak with people in this land,
    As they their goals pursue.

All people lived in friendliness,
    So there was only peace.
They fed on fruits and berries, then,
    So animals increased.

Three human groups were made by God.
    All differed by their hair.
The first had hair all over them,
    As if they were a bear.

The Wisdom of American Indian Mythology

The white man had hair on his face,
　His head and legs and arms.
But hair he had upon his face
　Did little for his charms.

The red man had hair on his head,
　Jet black and straight and long.
But he had none on face or chin,
　And thought hair there was wrong.

When hairy people disappeared,
　The white man grew more greedy.
He cried because his skin was pale
　And little eyes were beady.

God made the white man childish,
　And very selfish, too,
He cried and pouted all the time,
　Not knowing what to do.

So god's Great Spirit gave to him
　Some sticks with which to play.
Those sticks then turned into a horse,
　Which man still rides today.

The Wisdom of American Indian Mythology

The white man with his bearded face,
　　Though pale in need of sunning,
Was judged by red men like the wolf,
　　Too tricky and too cunning.

Whites wrote their promises with smoke
　　Which curled, then went aloft.
So everything agreed upon,
　　Quite soon just drifted off.

One hand would give a friendly gift,
　　The other take it back.
In this way white men all became
　　Land-grabbing maniacs.

Their leaders had two sets of ears,
　　For red man and for white.
They closed or opened as they pleased,
　　Ignoring red man's plight.

The white man also talked too much
　　But seldom spoke the truth.
So is it any wonder then,
　　Deceit passed to his youth.

Through hostages both races tried
  To change the lives each led.
Some tried to make the red men white,
  And white men into red.

When captured Indians were freed,
  They fled back to their tribe.
They could not live the white man's life
  Nor do what whites prescribed.

But captured whites saw values that
  All Indians held dear.
That they would choose to stay with them,
  Is obviously clear.

Whites knew they'd cheated Indians
  And stole ancestral land.
The values red men cherished
  Most whites found contraband.

The prisoners loved freedom now
  Found in captivity.
The silence of the lonely woods,
  Seemed like festivity.

The clothes and styles they treasured once
    Had little meaning now.
For they were all external things,
    Which muddled lives somehow.

And like red men these whites soon learned
    The land is yours and mine.
So pitch your tent and move about.
    And do not be confined.

The whole world is a gift from God,
    Enjoy it while you can.
Learn to relax and live in peace,
    And love your fellow man.

These captives were adopted by
    New families and tribe.
New brothers and new sisters now
    Were standing by their side.

They loved this new life they now led.
    And if they were set free,
They soon escaped back to the tribe,
    For there they wished to be.

The Wisdom of American Indian Mythology

The white man could not understand
    How this could come about.
But if he were abducted once,
    He knew without a doubt.

Perhaps, we all are Indians,
    At least within our heart,
For things we think we treasure now
    We know will soon depart.

For as we age, we gather in
    The wisdom of the wise.
The things we cherished in our youth,
    With age we analyze.

It's then we see they cannot give,
    The things we hoped they would.
It's then we also wonder how
    We ever thought they could.

Kachina doll
Private collection

THE ORIGIN OF THE DOG

The God Magician made the world,
    But something wasn't right.
There were a lot of animals,
    But no men were in sight.

He then determined to make man,
    And formed him out of clay.
He built a stove and gathered wood
    To cook the clay that day.

While God Magician gathered wood,
    Coyote stood around.
He took the clay and changed the shape,
    Until he formed a hound.

Man-maker then fired up the stove,
    Without the least delay.
And when the oven was red hot,
    He put inside the clay.

When it was done, he breathed in life.
    And took it from the heat.
It barked a lot and wagged its tail,
    And peed upon man's feet.

Magician saw coyote's hand
    And knew this was his trick.
And so Magician cooked one more,
    But took it out too quick.

It was a man, but far too pale,
    He looked like he was sick.
And that's how white man came to be,
    He left the heat too quick.

Man-maker made another form
    Which this time cooked too long.
It was a man, but far too dark,
    So something must be wrong.

That's how the black man came to be.
    He just got overcooked.
He was too long upon the heat
    At least that's how he looked.

The timing was coyote's fault.
    Both times he called out "when."
This time he would time things himself
    And so he tried again.

Man-maker timed things perfectly.
 And certainly it shows.
As he took from the oven's heat
 The first of all Pueblos.

I'm sure each tribe thinks it's the best,
 Though others might disclaim.
Each boast makes things more challenging,
 And makes of life a game.

Apache basket design
Museum of the American Indian
Heye Foundation, NY

WHY GRIZZLIES WALK
ON ALL FOURS

There was a time when grizzly bears
    Walked upright and could talk.
But that was when the Sky Chief ruled
    The skies through which he walked.

The weather was too cold above
    And so he came below.
But first he formed a mountain top
    Then made a path through snow.

When half way down he dug some holes
    And trees began to sprout.
Then from his footprints in the snow
    Came mountain streams and trout.

He broke off pieces from his cane
    To cast into the stream.
First beavers and then otters came
    As part of Sky Chief's scheme.

The smaller pieces swam like fish
    And that's what they became.
Then falling leaves were turned to birds,
    But no two were the same.

The big parts of his cane were used
　　To make all other beasts.
The largest was the grizzly bear
　　That Sky Chief's cane unleashed.

This bear was covered with long hair
　　And had sharp claws as feet.
He walked about like people did
　　And talked to those he'd meet.

He looked so fierce that Sky Chief sent
　　Him to the woods to live.
And in those woods he made his den
　　And dwelled a fugitive.

Now Sky Chief moved his family
　　Below to make their berth.
They lived beneath the mountain,
　　By which he climbed to earth.

He cut a hole in mountain's top
　　To let out all the smoke.
But when the wind blew very hard,
　　It served a counterstroke.

When smoke came back all eyes would burn,
    And tears began to flow.
The Sky Chief sent his daughter then
    To tell wind not to blow.

But first he warned her not to stick
    Her head through open hole.
A strong wind might blow her away
    And make her lose control.

She climbed a ladder to the top
    And warned the wind, "Beware."
But then she wished to see the sea,
    Which could be seen from there.

She poked her head above the hole,
    And caught the wind's full force.
She tumbled down the mountainside,
    Too swift for much remorse.

A grizzly found the frightened girl,
    And took her to his wife.
The wife raised her with other cubs,
    As she joined in their life.

She one day wed the eldest cub,
  And many children bore.
They didn't have the dark thick hair
  As bears all had before.

The grizzly who had mothered her
  Was now about to die.
But first she sought forgiveness,
  For living out a lie.

She sent her oldest grandson bear
  To Sky Chief's catacomb,
To tell him where his daughter was
  So he could take her home.

He hurried down the mountainside
  Perturbed at bear's charade.
It wasn't right that there should be
  A race he had not made.

His fierce frown killed the mother bear.
  He cursed the bears she bore.
"Get down upon your hands and knees
  And walk upon all four."

"And you will never talk again
  For this misdeed you did.
A growl will be your only noise.
  All speech I now forbid."

He put his daughter on his back,
  And left for who knows where.
Some say he went back to the sky
  In flight from loathsome bear.

The grandsons of the Sky Chief, then,
  Became the world's first braves.
They still will not kill grizzly bears,
  Or send them to their graves.

For Indians descended from
  That grizzly who played nurse.
They are somehow related yet,
  In spite of Sky Chief's curse.

Some men today still poke their head
  Where it does not belong.
And when they do, they're blown about,
  For worldly winds are strong.

They're carried from their sheltered homes
    To wed some grizzly bear,
Which means the spirit of the age,
    Which seemed so debonair.

Men are deceived and thus content,
    To be what they are not.
And though their lives are all mixed up,
    They think it's Camelot.

But comes the day of reckoning,
    When Sky Chief grows aware.
He curses every passing fad,
    Depicted as this bear.

Yes, curiosity killed the cat!
    But what's the lesson here?
Don't horse around with grizzly bears
    To further your career.

Navajo sand painting
Wheelwright Museum of the American Indian, Santa Fe

DEATH AND BURIAL RITES

A common misconception about American Indians is that they are all more or less the same. Because we see common references to shamans and vision quests, to war dances and healing rituals, to peace pipes and powwows, we are inclined to lump all Native Americans together into a single animistic system of beliefs, ignoring the fact that there were many hundreds of distinct cultures and customs native to America.

Indian tribal religion was not a personal relationship between the deity and the individual. It was rather a covenant between God and a particular community. Religious activity was tribal activity--its legends, beliefs, and ceremonies. Religion dominated the tribal culture. Political activity and religious activity were not distinguishable. There could be no salvation apart from the continuance of the tribe. Doctrine was not needed and so there were no heresies. Theology was a communal experience and needed no elaboration or articulation. The only sin was not to participate in community affairs.

Since each community was different, so also was each tribal religion. The Indian did not so much live in the tribe as the tribe lived in him. All Indians saw the journey of life as a single spiritual journey. That journey moved from one religious rite of passage to another; from the passage rite of birth to the passage rite of naming; from the passage rite of puberty to the passage rite of marriage. Finally there was the passage rite of death. The beliefs and practices surrounding these important ritual moments differed greatly in the hundreds of tribes that made up the Native Indian population, each with its own complexity of language, custom, history, and mythology. It is not surprising, then, that there was a wide variety of beliefs concerning the notion of death among the many tribes of North America. Nor is it at all surprising that there were also some common elements in those beliefs.

Pueblos buried their dead facing the rising sun. Sun Father was the giver and taker of life. What He gave, He eventually took back. Pueblos were involved in the worship of ancestors, who at death became Cloud People or lesser gods. Even dead enemies were transformed into rainmaking spirits. This transformation took place through a scalping ceremony. Among the Hopi, wicked enemies were believed to undergo punishment after death. Dead witches became mere smoke and thus could not join the Cloud People.

Some Indians were buried in a flexed position looking west, the traditional place of the happy hunting ground. The Sioux happy hunting ground was a place where warriors rode magnificent steeds through the sky. The Algonquins considered the dead hero, the divine Chipiapoos, protector of the Land of the Dead and the Guardian of Souls. When Tewas died, relatives dressed the corpse. Moccasins were reversed as would everything be in the next life. Tewas believed that the dead went to a place of "endless cicada singing." Little attention was given to death, however, in Navaho beliefs. Their religion was a religion of life. The Navaho had no concept of a life following death in which the dead joined their gods in some vague happy hunting ground. Their vague idea of an afterlife was like an unpleasant limbo.

Other tribes believed that the souls of the dead wandered about the world in the company of their ancestors for four days following death. During those four days, the relatives lived in mortal fear that a lonely soul might return to take one of them along for companionship. On the fourth night, relatives of the deceased held a releasing rite. The bowl, used at birth in the naming ceremony of the deceased, was now broken. The living could then relax. They washed and ate and returned to their normal routine. The departed soul was now at rest.

Most Indians believed that death came when the soul departed the body. There was no fear of death among Indians, for death was considered a part of the order of nature. Life would follow death as surely as wave would follow wave upon the sea.

The famous Chief Joseph spoke the following words to his subjects:

> "My body is returning to my mother earth and my spirit is going very soon to see the Great Spirit Chief."

Chief Seattle taught the same:

> "The white man will never be alone. Let him be just and deal kindly with my people, for the dead are not powerless. Dead, did I say? There is no death, only a change of worlds."

Death was not considered a condition of formless and homeless spirits, but an ordered and purposeful creation in which the dead merely made a passage from one form of existence to another. The ancestors of the deceased came to meet him and take him with them. Some tribes dressed their dead in fur and feathers, faces were painted, necklaces and headdress were placed upon the deceased. They were then placed on a litter or burial mound. Special grave offerings were buried with the dead to assist them in the next life, like bows and arrows, pipes, flint knives, jewelry, and shell rattles. Often a pet dog was killed and buried with the dead to welcome him to his new life. Among the Natchez Indians of Mississippi, when a tribal chief died, his wives were killed and buried with him. In many ways, death was looked upon as a continuation of this life.

In some tribes, widows cut their hair and blackened their faces. They wore rags and shunned all company for up to a year. They could not remarry until their former mother-in-law granted the proper permission. Respect for the dead was of paramount importance among all Indians.

Other tribes cremated the body on a funeral pyre shortly after death. Prior to cremation the body was placed upon a rack and suspended between the sky and earth to be closer to the sun. Some tribes buried their dead, but without a box or a coffin, although the dead were sometimes placed in a log that had been hollowed out by fire. The name of the deceased was never mentioned again. The corpse was never looked upon. That's why burial was so soon after death. If a person died inside a teepee, the teepee was ceremonially burned along with all the deceased's belongings.

Indian religions focused on the traditions of their ancestors. Ashes of the deceased were sacred and their resting place was hallowed ground. How cruel were those whites who desecrated Indian burial grounds or forced tribes to abandon their ancestors by relocating whole tribes thousands of miles away from those burial grounds forever!

Cochita pottery design
Southwest Museum, Los Angeles

THE COYOTE CAUSES DEATH

When man was first brought forth by God,
  He never was to die.
But men became so plentiful,
  That things soon went awry.

There wasn't room to move about.
  The world was far too crowded,
For since no one had heard of death,
  No one was ever shrouded.

The chiefs assembled to decide
  What Indians should do.
Most thought that man should die awhile,
  And then come back like new.

All voted for a short-term death,
  Except the mean coyote.
When men wrote their bereavement plan,
  He wrote his own footnote.

The coyote thought man's plan absurd.
  His own plan was more clever.
He thought death should be permanent.
  Yes, death should last forever.

The Wisdom of American Indian Mythology

The whole wide world would be too small,
  If population grew.
And surely food would be too scarce
  To feed Cheyenne and Sioux.

But all the others disagreed.
  "Forever" was too long.
Since they would miss their relatives,
  The heartless wolf was wrong.

Then shamans built a large grass house,
  Which myths have not ignored.
When songs were sung the dead would come,
  To have their life restored.

So when at last there was a death,
  The songs prescribed were sung.
A whirlwind then began to blow,
  And over grass house hung.

When spirit's soul, borne by this wind,
  Came to the open door,
The coyote quickly slammed it shut,
  As wind began to roar.

So when its entry was denied,
  The whirlwind sped away.
And death was thus eternalized,
  As it still is today.

And since the door of life was closed,
  Dead spirits still will roam,
Until they find the path that leads
  To spirits' tranquil home.

The mean coyote then rushed away,
  For men detested him.
You'll see him constantly look back,
  For men in quest of him.

No one will feed or shelter him.
  Men rather seek his life.
For due to coyote's shamelessness,
  Death comes and brings forth strife.

One wonders what life would be like,
  If coyote had agreed
With all the other Indians
  And what they had decreed.

Death would be like vacationing,
  Withdrawal from routine.
It could be fun as we would meet,
  The new and unforeseen.

But there could be some problems, too,
  When we came back to life.
Perhaps some Indian would be
  Now wedded to our wife.

So maybe things are not all bad
  As coyote has arranged them.
Those now in happy hunting grounds,
  I'm sure would not exchange them.

So live as man was meant to live.
  And die as death should be.
And then you'll find that neither one
  Is a catastrophe.

I think that red men knew this well,
  That's why they had no fear.
They lived the truths that they professed,
  Though death was always near.

The white men thought them savages.
　　The opposite was true.
Admission of white ruthlessness
　　Is longtime overdue.

Who stole whose land, who killed whose game?
　　Who made and broke their pacts?
Who confiscated tribal lands
　　For reservation tracts?

What white men could not understand
　　They thought should be destroyed.
White history hides injustices,
　　Deceitfulness deployed.

All wisdom has its limits.
　　Stupidity has none.
Some claim it peaked in Custer,
　　That madman with a gun.

Sikyatki pottery design
Southwest Museum
Los Angeles

LOVE IN THE FACE OF DEATH

Although a brave loved his new wife,
    His mother hated her.
So while her son was hunting game,
    She terminated her.

She placed a pointed object where
    Her daughter-in-law would squat.
And when the wife sat on that point,
    She died upon the spot.

A funeral pyre was then prepared,
    A hot one, it's presumed.
For by the time the brave returned,
    The body was consumed.

The saddened brave went to the pyre
    And sat there in a trance.
Then curls of dust rose from the ash,
    As if to do a dance.

At last, one larger than the rest
    Whirled all about, then rose.
It took off whirling down the path,
    For heaven, I suppose.

The brave then set off after it,
    As it went down the road.
That night he saw it was his wife
    In search of death's abode.

She headed for the barren rocks,
    Past which all dead must go.
There if their lives had not been good,
    Rocks dealt a crushing blow.

She then informed her loving spouse,
    Where she went, he could not.
For life and death are opposites,
    In spite of their love's knot.

He told his wife he could not live,
    If she were not his queen.
She placed him then upon her back,
    So he would not be seen.

They traveled till they came unto
    The River of the Dead.
They made the risky crossing and
    Continued on ahead.

They journeyed on until they met
    Her parents and her kin.
Then all her friends who died before,
    Now greeted her again.

Most were not pleased a live man came
    Into the Land of Dead.
But since the two were so in love,
    Complaints were left unsaid.

The brave had need of special food
    For his live appetite.
And with the eyes he brought from earth
    He only saw at night.

One day while on a spirit hunt,
    The spirits shouted: "Game."
Since it was day, he could not see,
    And so he couldn't aim.

By chance or luck he killed two deer
    As they passed by to graze.
So after this accomplishment,
    He won the people's praise.

The spirit hearts reached out to him
    And also to his bride.
Why should they have to live like this,
    Since he had not yet died?

The dead shades thought it best for them
    To live with living men.
And so they left the Land of Death
    To live on earth again.

Before they left, the spirits warned
    That once among the living,
For three days they must live apart,
    A sign of their thanksgiving.

Obediently, these lovers spent
    Three days and nights apart.
But on the fourth day they embraced,
    And loved with all their heart.

Unhappily, they did not know
    Dead shades keep different time.
Three days meant three years to the dead,
    So their love was a crime.

Next morning he awoke to find
    His wife not by his side.
The spirit world had called her back.
    Its laws had been defied.

This spirit world seems rather cruel,
    The way it acted here,
Concocting its own calendar,
    Which surely wasn't clear.

How could this brave know dead man's time?
    He was among the living!
It seems to me the dead could be
    A little more forgiving.

I guess there'll be surprises when
    You enter Land of Dead.
Their counting is confusing,
    Especially if you're wed.

Hohokam art
Arizona State Museum, University of Arizona, Tuscon

THE CHOICE OF LIFE OR DEATH

Was something missing from the world,
    That Old Man Maker made?
And if it were, what could it be,
    That failed to make the grade?

There was no woman in the world,
    Nor was there girl or boy.
This was quite strange, for what could bring
    The world more love or joy?

The Old Man knew this was a flaw,
    As all men would agree,
For life could never be complete
    Until they came to be.

Till there were women in the world
    Young children could not be.
For kids are not brought by the stork,
    Or dispatched C.O.D.

Old Man Creator then resolved,
    To remedy his flaw.
He'd make a woman right away
    So man could have a squaw.

What should a woman's shape look like?
    Creator didn't know.
He made some samples out of clay
    To see which way to go.

At last a woman and her child
    Seemed pleasing to his sight.
Creator looked upon them both
    And saw they were just right.

But they were not alive as yet.
    They were but lifeless clay.
Old Man then set about to bring
    Them to the light of day.

By his command they first sat up
    And then began to walk.
He led them to the river's bank
    And there taught them to talk.

The woman then began to speak:
    "What do you call our state,
That we can walk and breathe and eat
    And even cogitate?"

"Your state is life," Creator said.
  "Before you were just clay.
But now you live by my decree
  Which I declared today."

"But what were we before we lived?
  I must not be misled."
"Before you lived," he answered her,
  "You were completely dead."

"Will we now live forever more,
  Or will we soon be dead?"
"I never once considered it,"
  Old Man Creator said.

"I guess I should decree right now
  An answer you can quote.
Soon after death you'll come to life,
  If bison chips will float."

I'll throw one in this running brook,
  And it can then portend.
If that chip floats upon the top,
  Your life will have no end.

"But chips dissolve," the woman said,
    "I'd rather use a stone.
We'll live forever, if it floats,
    If not, life's just on loan."

The woman had just come alive
    And knew but very little.
She didn't know that stones would sink,
    Nor bison chips were brittle.

She cast a stone into the stream.
    It sank before her eye.
"You made your choice," the Old Man said,
    "All humans now must die."

Herein we see the Bible's Eve
    Still choosing death to life.
But even though she messed things up,
    At least man had a wife.

Too bad she didn't choose the dung
    In preference to the stone.
Our lives would be less stressful now,
    And death would be unknown.

But even though her choice was poor,
  She has been compensated.
As she gives birth and hands life on
  Somehow death is negated.

Her value is quite manifold,
  As she perfects the earth.
Not only does she cause its life
  But most things which have worth.

She teaches children how to live,
  And thereby teaches man.
And this is how its always been
  Since life on earth began.

Though her first choice on earth was wrong,
  And issued forth death's call,
Her dignity has been restored
  And she is loved by all.

Acoma pottery design
Southwest Museum, Los Angeles

MAN'S BEST FRIEND

The Plains Sioux had a lovely myth
    Why dogs are man's best friend.
It's one of many oral myths
    The Sioux have left unpenned.

Once animals and men were one
    And lived in peace on earth.
They spoke each other's language then
    And had done so from birth.

But God in time reversed his plans
    For animals and man.
Man by his reason was to rule
    And gain the upper hand.

God said that they should live apart,
    Pursuing their own ends.
And this is what they since have done
    And are no longer friends.

God drew a line and dug a ditch
    Then called out to creation
To take the side assigned to them
    And live in separation.

The animals went to the left,
While man went to the right.
And then the ditch began to grow
In width and depth and height.

These animals were now content
To live apart from man.
They headed for the wilderness
And in the forest ran.

But as the ditch was widening,
The loyal dog looked back.
He couldn't leave the man he loved
And so retraced his track.

He ran and leaped across the ditch
And did it just in time,
For soon its banks were far too steep
For man or beast to climb.

And since that day the dog has been
The faithful friend of man.
No other beast has shown such love,
And there is none that can.

The two are somehow seen as one,
 Man and his faithful friend.
And this will always be the case
 Until the world will end.

How foolish is that man who draws,
 A line upon the sand,
And says no one should cross that line
 To offer him a hand.

What blessing that man misses!
 What friendships have been lost!
His independence is preserved,
 But is it worth the cost?

Some think they are an island
 Within the human sea.
But they are disillusioned
 In thinking they are free.

In many ways they're slaves to selves,
 Though this they won't admit.
They'll never know another's love
 Or share another's wit.

They miss the joys a friend can give,
    If friend be but a dog.
They've doomed themselves to loneliness
    And foolish monologue.

And so the wise man will erase
    Those lines drawn in the sand,
For other friends we must embrace
    If life is to expand.

In doing this we take a chance,
    For others can cause pain.
But if we do not take that chance,
    There's nothing we can gain.

For life is not a negative,
    The absence of caprice.
It's rather something positive
    Like love and joy and peace.

Laguna drinking vessel
Museum of Indian Art and Culture, Santa Fe

A NATION'S GREATEST SHAME

Most of us are slow to give up the preconceived ideas of American Indians that we garnered from the fiction of western novels and Hollywood movies that most often depicted Indians as cruel barbarians attacking innocent wagon trains. That same mistaken perception of American Indians is still promulgated today in grade school history books that depict all settlers as generous, kind, and self-sacrificing and all Indians as inhuman, dishonest, and treacherous. These childish text books portray Pontiac, Tecumseh, Black Hawk, Manuelito; and Sitting Bull, Crazy Horse, and Chief Joseph as villains instead of patriots, equal in devotion to their way of life as was Washington or Lincoln. These Indian leaders simply tried to prevent the rape of their land by strangers who were more strong, more greedy and infinitely more ruthless.

Throughout the 19th century, the white man sought to tame the "wild west." The red man did not consider the open plains, the rolling hills and the winding rivers of his native land a wild wilderness that needed to be tamed. The land had been inherited from his ancestors and offered him everything he needed for peace, happiness, and survival. The colonists, however, wanted for their own use that land which Indians had held sacred for centuries and whites had few qualms in taking it. It seems that colonists everywhere have always rationalized what they take by force from any country's original inhabitants.

Canada stole land from native Indians; Australia stole land from the Aborigines; Brazil practiced genocide against the indigenous population of that country; Sweden invaded the land of the Lapps. And almost from the beginning, the English, Dutch, and French colonists all but exterminated the American Indians in their unending greed to confiscate the land these Indians possessed from time immemorial. The betrayal of the American Indian has been and will always be our national shame. No minority has been more abused or more cruelly mistreated. Indians were deprived of a homeland and a foreseeable future. This is where the west was lost, though few will admit it.

In face of the unceasing advancement of white men, the Indian people seemed to be orphans who could look nowhere for help. At the time of the Civil War there were about 31 million whites. There were just over 300 thousand Indians. Whatever the white man wanted the white man took. Treaties that were made became treaties that were broken. Most often negotiations were made by bribe and by whiskey.

When Indians suffered hunger and even starvation due to the indiscriminate buffalo slaughter by whites, the contemptible Andrew Myrick said of the Dakota Sioux in 1862: "Let them eat grass or their own dung."

White civilization drove the red man from his home he loved. It often tortured or killed him, but the white man could never make the red man his slave. There were hundreds of Indian tribes and nations that inhabited this land and all were exploited either by the colonists or by the federal government that came after them. The story of the Cherokee is the story of every tribe east of the Mississippi with changes only in detail.

The title of Cherokee people to their land is the most ancient, pure, and absolute known to man. Its date is beyond the reach of human memory. Its validity was confirmed by possession and enjoyment antecedent to all pretense and claim to the contrary.

Cherokee existed as a distinct nation for a period extending into antiquity beyond the date and records and memory of man. Those attributes had never been relinquished by the Cherokee and cannot be dissolved by the expulsion of that nation from its territory by the powers of the United States government.

In 1754, the British Crown took over from the colonies all policies dealing with Indians. It did this to protect the Indians from the greed of the colonists. Each tribe was considered an independent nation. A tribe's right to its land was considered inalienable except through voluntary surrender. Any attempt by colonists to deprive Indians of their land was illegal. This stipulation increased the hatred of colonists for the Crown. This is why the Cherokee, the largest Iroquoian tribe, sided with the British during the Revolution.

In 1828, the Cherokee Nation still held seven million acres in Georgia, North Carolina, and Tennessee. When gold was discovered in Georgia, Andrew Jackson forced all Indians to move west of the Mississippi by the Indian Removal Act of 1830. The Georgia legislature then annexed all Cherokee land. A lottery was held to distribute that land to whites. The Cherokee appealed to the Supreme Court, which ruled that the Cherokee were not a foreign nation. The Court later reversed itself and said Cherokee were a nation and no one could take their land. "A weaker government does not surrender its independence by association with a stronger one." Jackson, who had an uncontrollable animosity toward Indians, said of the Court: "John Marshall has rendered his decision, now let him enforce it." It was almost with contempt that Georgia and the federal government continued its policies of greed and lust for land toward the Cherokee.

In 1838, General Scott invaded and burned villages, captured Indians and gave their livestock to whites. The Indians were sent to Arkansas. Of the 14,000 Indians forced to walk those many miles 100 died daily. A total of 4000 perished on this journey which has come to be called "The Trail of Tears."

In December of that year President Van Buren reported to Congress the "happy effects of the Cherokee removal without any apparent reluctance. The liquidation of all Indians became the formalized policy, law, and practice of the United States government. The full intensity of that policy lasted most of the 19th century. It was executed by the military under the leadership of such men as Sherman and Sheridan and the incompetent and arrogant Custer, a buffoon who thought that war was no place for a gentleman, unless he were seated upon a horse.

Later on, in spite of a past Supreme Court decision, Grant decreed that Indian tribes were not independent nations but wards of the federal government. This made Indians second class citizens by law as they had always been by fact. Is it any wonder that Indians thought the tongues of white men were forked like the viper. So often white men came under the guise and pretense of friendship only to lead the red man down the path of ruin and complete destruction. Cochise, the famed Apache Chief, said of whites: "None is more treacherous than the Americans and none more arrogant."

General Francis Walker, Commissioner of Indian Affairs in 1871, sought to justify the United States policies of intrigue by the following statement: "When dealing with savage men as with savage beasts, no question of national honor can arise. Whether to fight, to run away, or to employ a ruse is solely a question of expediency."

Beginning in 1870, the United States aimed to eliminate the Plains Indians by a series of subterfuges. Homesteaders swarmed over the land that had been promised to Indian tribes for "as long as the grass grows and the rivers run." Military assaults were continually made on Indian encampments. The government exploited tribal rivalries so Indians would kill Indians. The very lifeline of Indian society was threatened with the random destruction of the buffalo by white hunters. Treaties were made and broken. Indians were imprisoned on reservations. Indian leaders were deprived of any tribal authority. Indian children were placed in white boarding schools to Americanize them. Many Indian customs and practices were banned by white man's law.

Such white arrogance brought on many wars with the Plains Indians. By 1892, these Indian Wars ceased. The Indian had been broken. His religion had been killed. His land had been stolen. His forests had been clear cut. His spirit had been crushed.

Unfortunately, most Americans look upon this period of their history with pride. It was rather a period of terrible shame and will one day demand its own compensation, at least in the spirit of this Pawnee proverb: "Do not kill or injure your neighbor, for it is not him that you injure. You injure yourself." Chief Running Bear said of white men: "The man from Europe is still a foreigner and an alien. And he still hates the man who questioned his path across the continent."

Indians will never accept a meaningless brotherhood of man that does away with the distinction between races and maintains that society must be homogenous. The Indian is too proud of his heritage, and rightly so.

THE COMING OF THE WHITE MAN

Iktome was the Spiderman,
   The bearer of bad news.
All tribes could understand his speech,
   From Pawnee to the Sioux.

He was a clever trickster,
   As spider or as man.
And he could change to either one,
   Depending on his plan.

One day he came into a camp
   And shouted out this warning:
"New kinds of men will soon appear,
   With ruthlessness alarming."

"They'll be like me, a trickster,
   A liar and a thief.
They'll steal and overrun your land
   And cause all red men grief."

Iktome called a court of war,
   With every chief on hand.
He asked that each advise his tribe
   To guard its native land.

The Wisdom of American Indian Mythology

Iktome, then, climbed up a hill,
    Attended by great crowds.
He wove a web into the sky
    And climbed into the clouds.

The Spiderman next visited
    The nations of the Sioux,
To warn of coming hopeless days,
    When things would go askew.

Seashells brought him this message
    To spread throughout the land,
To warn red men that white-boned men
    Would soon be in command.

"They're coming from across the sea
    To steal your paradise.
And when you see foreboding signs,
    You must not close your eyes."

"These long-legged and white-boned men
    Will not be wise, but clever.
They're coming here to steal the land
    Which you have held forever."

"Their long legs will be filled with greed,
And lies will mark their track.
Please make this message widely known
To stop this white attack."

Iktome wove another web,
Then took a spider's form,
To spread this message everywhere
Before the violent storm.

He journeyed to the Blue Cloud tribes,
Known as Arapaho,
To warn them of white-boned men's greed
That soon would cause them woe.

"They're coming soon and they'll devour
All nations in their way.
They will destroy the earth itself.
Your rights they will betray."

They asked for signs so they could know,
While whites were still afar.
"They will be here when red men see
A double shining star."

Again Iktome disappeared,
    Then journeyed to the Crow.
He spoke their tongue quite fluently,
    As red men's nuncio.

"These White Long-legs are coming soon
    To steal the things you love,
The grass and trees and animals,
    And birds that fly above."

"They'll ask of you a different life,
    But don't forego your past.
Don't throw away the things you've learned,
    But hold to them steadfast."

The Crow chiefs asked the Spiderman:
    "Why must White Long-legs come?
We do not want them in our land
    To cause our martyrdom."

"But whether you want them or not,
    The Whites," he said, "would come.
They'll soon arrive here from the east,
    To form their rascaldom."

"When these men come and ask for land,
　　You always must say, 'No.'
Please, bring this message everywhere,
　　So every tribe will know."

The Spiderman then told the Crow:
　　"Like rocks, you'll last forever.
The white ash tree revealed to me,
　　Whites are not wise, but clever."

The Crows then fed Iktome
　　Some berries mixed with fat.
He thanked them and was on his way
　　To spread his caveat.

The Crow chiefs stood before their tents,
　　War-bonnets on their heads.
And then they saw Iktome weave
　　And climb these new spun threads.

He went to the Shoshone tribes
　　And they, too, heard his cries:
"The white long-legged men will come
　　And fill your heads with lies."

The chief of the Shoshone tribes
    Placed sticks upon the ground.
One pointing north, one pointing south,
    These white men to confound.

Shoshone did not want new things.
    The things they had were good.
But they were told new things would come
    And could not be withstood.

He next went to the Pawnee tribes
    And shouted his alarm
About impending evil things,
    Of sickness, ills, and harm.

He then returned unto the Sioux,
    As spider on a thread.
He warned the Sioux the time was near
    When they would be misled.

"How will these new men come to us?"
    The Sioux asked Spiderman.
"They'll disembark from wooden boats
    And come upon your land."

"These men will lie and cheat and steal.
    Their pride will try to shame you.
They'll try to make you like themselves.
    They even will rename you."

"When will they come?" the Sioux chief asked,
    "We'd surely like to know."
"You'll know," he said, "when you see killed
    Great herds of buffalo."

"They'll spread among you evil things
    Like prejudice and hate,
Like plagues and common treachery,
    Your courage to abate."

"They'll try to take away your God.
    I know this, and I fear it.
They'll seek to wipe out Tanka's creed
    To rob you of Great Spirit."

"They'll come and live within your midst,
    And claim to be your friend.
But do not trust them in the least;
    Their lies will never end."

When Sioux then asked: "Is there no hope?"
  He uttered on the spot:
"If grass and trees will speak to them
  The truths white men forgot."

"If white men love what red men love,
  And learn what red men know.
If white men treasure nature's gifts,
  Perhaps your trust can grow."

"But do not place much hope in this,
  For white men never learn.
Their lust for land will always be
  Their only great concern."

"What they don't steal, they will destroy
  If it is in their way.
So always heed this warnings, then,
  That you have heard today."

Then Iktome, the Spiderman,
  Left all the tribes he'd warned.
But soon those red men all forgot
  Those things they later mourned.

It wasn't long till white men came
    With black hats, boots, and clothes,
With pale white skin and bluish eyes,
    And hair beneath their nose.

They spoke a language no one knew,
    And no one knew their source.
They rode upon the strangest beast
    That they had named the "horse."

Some men among them held a cross;
    The others held a gun,
Which shot out flames and made great noise,
    And killed men on the run.

White sickness spread among the tribes,
    And took lives everywhere.
The red man's lands were stolen,
    And white courts did not care.

The Trail of Tears and Wounded Knee
    Should rip white pride to shreds.
The arrogance of Custer
    Should make whites hang their heads.

Such treatment of the Indians
    Was baseness unsurpassed,
Which must cry out for equity
    As long as time will last.

I don't know how white men can make
    The restitution needed.
But history proves that lands they have
    Were never justly deeded.

Such wrongful crimes of countrymen
    True history should proclaim.
And when it does, we'll all agree,
    It is our country's shame.

Pueblo jewelry
Museum of New Mexico, Santa Fe

CONCLUSION

It's not enough to hang our heads.
     We must make right our wrong,
For sorrow without recompense
     Has gone on far too long.

 The individual cannot solve
     A nation's avarice.
The government alone can solve
     A problem such as this.

Nor should it use those structures now
     That blundered in the past,
Whose work with Indian Affairs
     Made errors unsurpassed.

It must consult with Indians
     To know their wants and needs,
To make up for its past mistakes
     And many past misdeeds.

It cannot let a culture die,
     Nor let it fade away.
It must promote and keep alive
     The wealth of yesterday.

And if we fail a second time,
    Whom do we have to blame?
Will it be our forefathers or
    Ourselves who bear the shame?

I think we know the answer that
    We white men have to give.
And if we answer with our heart,
    The red men might forgive.

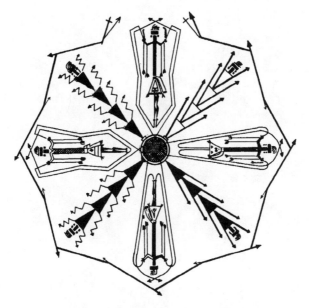

Navajo sand painting--Mountain Shooting
Wheelwright Museum of the American Indian, Santa Fe

BIBLIOGRAPHY

Andrist, Ralph. The Long Death; The Last Days of The Plains Indians, New York: McMillan, 1964.

Britt, Albert. Great Indian Chiefs, New York: Whittlesey House, 1938.

Brown, Dee. Bury My Heart At Wounded Knee, New York: Henry Holt Co., 1991.

Burland, Cottie. North American Indian Mythology, England: Hamlyn Publishing, 1973.

Catlin, George. North American Indians, England, 1856.

Clark, E.E. Indian Legends of the Pacific Northwest, Massachusetts: Cambridge University Press, 1958.

Davis, Britton. The Truth About Geronimo, Illinois: Lakeside Press, 1951.

Debo, Angie. A History of the Indians of the United States, Oklahoma: University of Oklahoma Press, 1970.

Deloria, Vine. Custer Died For Your Sins, New York: Avon, 1969.

Deloria, Vine. God Is Red, New York: Grosset & Dunlop, 1973.

Deloria, Vine. Behind the Trail of Broken Treaties, New York: Delacorte, 1974.

Erdoes, Richard. American Indian Myths and Legends, New York: Pantheon Books, 1984.

Ewers, John. Indian Life On The Upper Missouri, Oklahoma: University of Oklahoma Press, 1968.

Fleischer, Jane, Pontiac Chief of the Ottawas, New Jersey: Troll Associates.

Gattuso, John. Native America, Singapore: Hofer Press, 1991.

Graham, W.A. The Custer Myth, Pennsylvania: Stackpole, 1953.

Grinnell, George. The Fighting Cheyennes, Oklahoma: University of Oklahoma Press, 1956.

Heard, Isaac. History of the Siouz War, New York: Harper, 1864.

Horan, James. McKenney-Hall Portrait Gallery of American Indians, New York: Bramhall House, 1986.

Hultkranz, Ake. Native Religions of North America, New York: Harper Row, 1987.

Judson, Katharine. Myths and Legends of the Pacific North West, Illinois: McClurg, 1910.

Katz, William. Black Indians, New York: Atheneum, 1986.

Kraenzel, Carl. The Great Plains, Oklahoma: University of Oklahoma Press, 1955.

Leland, Godfrey. Algonquin Legends of New England, Massachusetts: Houghton Mifflin, 1884.

Marriott, Alice and Rachlin, Carol. Plains Indian Mythology, New York: Mentor Book, 1977.

Marriot, Alice and Rachlin, Carol, Peyote, New York: Signet, 1971.

McLaughlin, James. My Friend The Indian, Massachusetts: Houghton Mifflin, 1910.

Norman, Howard. How Glooskap Outwits Ice Giants, Massachusetts: Little, Brown, Co., 1989.

Oehler, C.M. The Great Sioux Uprising, New York: Oxford University Press, 1959.

Schmitt, Martin and Dee Brown. Fighting Indians of the West, New York: Scribner's, 1948.

Spence, Lewis. Myths and Legends of the North-American Indians, England: Harrap, 1914.

Sprague, Marshall. Massacre; The Tragedy At White River, Massachusetts: Little, Brown, 1957.

Talayesva, Don. <u>Sun Chief: The Autobiography of a Hopi Indian</u>, Connecticut: Yale University Press, 1942.

Wallace, Ernest and E. A. Hoebel. <u>The Comanches, Lords Of The South Plains</u>, Olkahoma: University of Oklahoma Press, 1952.

Wood, Charles. <u>A Book of Tales:Being Some Myths of the North American Indians</u>, New York: Vanguard, 1929.

INDEX

THE WISDOM OF AMERICAN INDIAN MYTHOLOGY
by John J. Ollivier

Discovering the colorful heritage and traditions of the American Indian forefathers has never been made more FUN, simple and easy-to-learn! Master storyteller John J. Ollivier captures Native American culture in prose and rhythm. The limericks help you to remember and learn the many delightful myths and tales-of-old. Each myth has a hidden or not-so-hidden gem of wisdom to share with all who will listen.

YOU WILL LEARN:
  *The origin of the Hopi Snake Dance
  * The origin of scalping
  * How healing began
  * The origin of the dog
  * The origin of the flute
  * The role of the woman in Indian life
  * The wisdom of proverbs from the major tribes

YOU WILL ENJOY THE METAPHORIC FABLES OF:
Why butterflies are silent; why grizzlies walk on all fours; why crows are black; why the coyote causes death; why bluebirds are blue; and the origin of mosquitoes.

The Wisdom of American Indian Mythology is not to be mistaken for a hard-edged approach to the study of culture. It is, however, an easy-to-understand, educational and genuinely unique and enjoyable exploration of little known Native American mythology.

ISBN 1-56087-049-4
Quality paperback with American Indian motifs,
272 pages
$17.95 plus $4.00 priority s/h

FUN WITH IRISH MYTHS
By John J. Ollivier

**A must for every Irishman
and those who have to
live with one!**

Fun With Irish Myths is a humorous and
valuable study of ancient Celtic tales,
myths and folklore written in an
encapturing style combining limerick
and prose. You will enjoy Ireland's little
known prehistory where Celtic gods and Irish heroes walked hand-
in-hand together in the realm of mythological fancy.

John Ollivier—teacher, counselor and master storyteller—acquaints
you with primitive tales and folklore. The myths are an effort to un-
derstand Irish heritage past, present and into the future.

With his unique insight of the Irish, Ollivier has taken a set of his-
torical circumstances and set his imaginative visions to rhyme—to
amuse, inform, and thoroughly entertain you. You will undoubtedly
find yourself among these pages!

Leprechauns, banshees and gods come to life... to entertain and de-
light. Everyone is proud of their heritage, perhaps none more so than
the Irish. And, since most of us can say that we are part Irish (espe-
cially on St. Patrick's Day), this book is a definite must—for every
Irishman... those who have to live with the Irish... and for those who
wish they were Irish!

ISBN 1-56087-014-1, LC# 91-11422
Quality paperback with Celtic illustrations, 192 pages
$11.95 plus $4.00 priority s/h

THE WISDOM OF AFRICAN MYTHOLOGY
by John J. Ollivier

NOMINATED FOR A PULITZER PRIZE

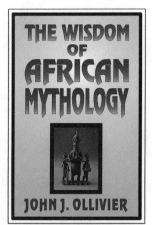

Authentic African folklore and folk tales. Passed down from generations of oral and written culture, these African tales-of-old are now shared in an entertaining, amusing and informative style. *The Wisdom of African Mythology is* a valuable asset to any home and can be a teaching tool in schools, universities, and colleges.

John J. Ollivier, master teacher, uses his special descriptive style of prose, and then creates easy-to-remember and humorous limericks. Ollivier has earned praise for his *Fun With Irish Myths, Fun With Greek Myths, Fun With Nordic Myths,* and his *Fun With Nursery Rhymes.*

You will enjoy the stories and legends. Discover the WISDOM in these African myths...

* The origin of death
* Why spiders have humps
* Why turtles have cracked shells
* The origins of fire
* God's first contact with man
* The origins of polyandry and polygamy

These are just a few of the legends, myths, and rhythm found in this dedicated and richly-woven work. Experience the African heritage.

ISBN# 1-56087-023-0, LC#91-35050
Quality paperback, 256 pages with African motifs
$14.95 plus $4.00 priority s/h

FOR FREE CATALOG
of over
100 HELPFUL books, audios,
CD-ROMs, computer programs

Write, Phone or Fax:
Top Of The Mountain Publishing
P.O. Box 2244
Pinellas Park, Florida
34664-2244 U.S.A.
Phone (813) 391-3843
Fax (813) 391-4598